SOCCER	John Callaghan
	University of Southern California
SWIMMING	Donald L. Gambril
	Harvard University
TENNIS, 3RD EDITION	Barry Pelton
	University of Houston
VOLLEYBALL	Randy Sandefur
	California State University, Long Beach
TOTAL FITNESS FOR MEN	J. Tillman Hall
	University of Southern California
TOTAL FITNESS FOR WOMEN	Emilyn Sheffield
	University of Southern California
SELF DEFENSE	Lynn M. Pacala
	Occidental College

3RD EDITION

TENNIS

BARRY C. PELTON
University of Houston

GOODYEAR PHYSICAL ACTIVITIES SERIES
EDITED BY J. TILLMAN HALL

Goodyear Publishing Company, Inc.
Santa Monica, California 90401

Library of Congress Cataloging in Publication Data

Pelton, Barry C
    Tennis.

    (Goodyear physical activities series)
    Bibliography: p.108
    1. Tennis.   I. Title.
GV995.P39 1980   796.34'2   79-21290
ISBN 0-87620-890-1

TENNIS
Barry C. Pelton
Third Edition

GOODYEAR PUBLISHING COMPANY, INC.
Santa Monica, California 90401
Y-8901-4

Current Printing (last digit):
10 9 8 7 6 5 4 3 2
Printed in the United States of America

ACKNOWLEDGMENTS

I played competitive tennis for about fifteen years. Throughout my athletic career, four people helped me immeasurably to develop skill and sportsmanship, and contributed to my interest in continued general education. I am grateful to a former teacher, Mrs. Rachel Calkins, and former coaches—Mr. Herschel Kimbrell, Mr. Alton Williams, and Dr. Perry Broom—for their confidence and support with respect to my playing ability and qualities as an individual. For aid in the preparation of this book I should like to thank Joy Hindman. To Mr. Ken Purdy, who did the photography, and to Nancy Harless, who did the illustrations, my sincere thanks. I also wish to extend my thanks to the models for the pictures: Wayne Diel, Jill Berenson, Kip Patterson, and Mary McCool of Louisiana State University. My thanks also to Karen Hausman, Valerie Wilkins, Melissa Zoelle, Robert Buchalter, Joel Hoffman, Paul Christian, and Dr. John Carley from the University of Houston for serving as models and doing the photography.

CONTENTS

EDITOR'S NOTE

TENNIS, by Barry Pelton, has been one of the most popular books for learning the basics of the game since 1969. Now, in this new third edition, Pelton brings you the latest information on skill aquisition, technique development, and tennis thinking, combined with his proven teaching concepts for learning this lifetime sport.

The book opens with a historical development of tennis that includes the great accomplishments and records of the game. This is followed by an introduction to the "language" of the game by a complete glossary of terms and a discussion of major team competitions and international championships. The chapter on equipment and facilities provides the latest information on player apparel (the advantage of certain fabrics used in tennis clothing, and types of footwear), rackets, strings, balls, courts, surfaces, and nets. A feature on the "Rules of Tennis" includes the new scoring procedure of sudden death tie breakers, 12—13 point tie breakers, and no-add systems.

At the heart of TENNIS, Third Edition, is the teaching of fundamental techniques and strategy. The chapter "Fundamental Strokes" teaches you in a careful, step-by-step progression, the basics of each tennis stroke, including the two handed forehand/backhand. This complete collection of shots is illustrated by how-to-do-it photographs. The discussion of strategy encompasses offensive and defensive play for both singles and doubles and includes "Warm-up do's and don'ts,"— a list of game preparation techniques essential to a winning strategy. "Measuring Improvement and Achievement" features an extensive review of the six most common faults in the game and what to do to correct them along with several drills and exercises designed to improve each aspect of your game. Conditioning hints and sports medicine are also included.

In "Beyond Basic Skills" you will learn how to develop power in your shots, add to your quickness and agility on the court, develop game etiquette and the art of being a good spectator. The last feature of the book, the "Performance Checklists," is perhaps its most helpful and practical aid. This series of checklists is designed to help you chart improvements in your performance and notice areas needing attention.

I highly recommend this thorough book to anyone interested in developing a good game of tennis.

BIOGRAPHY

Barry C. Pelton is Associate Professor in the Department of Health and Physical Education at the University of Houston. He holds an Ed.D. degree from the University of Southern California.

While an undergraduate, Dr. Pelton was a finalist in the doubles championships of the National Association of Intercollegiate Athletics. He also shared the national Mixed doubles title in the national Public Parks Tournament in 1962, and has defeated nationally and internationally ranked players.

TENNIS

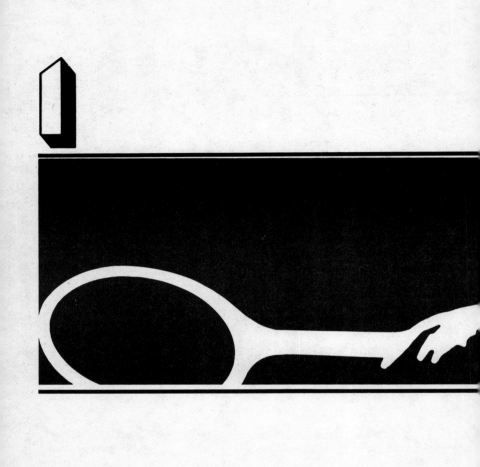

THE STORY OF TENNIS

WHY HISTORY?

The consideration of history per se is justifiable in the sense that it provides mankind with facts in a chronological order. It is refreshing to experience insight and perspective into the times, places, events, and real-life performances of other human beings. This experience enables one to throw his immediate concerns, in this case learning to play tennis, into a meaningful relationship or perspective with what has preceded.

Before considering the history of tennis, let us briefly touch on the history of physical education. Some

1

historians contend that physical education has neither a history nor a nature, but that at different periods of time people developed characteristic patterns of movement involving the human body and requiring the use of equipment. Hence, the basic materials involved in what is now "physical education" were the human body and its capacity to move and perform in various skills. Further, developing ability to move and perform may change an individual's way of perceiving his environment as well as his value system. Physical education and the impact of history may have different effects on each participant. Each sport which accrues as a part of contemporary physical education may do the same. The history of tennis is important in the sense that it enables the student to reflect upon *what* has happened and *why* it happened. With this picture imprinted, the focus then returns to the individual and how he may gain insight on himself in a historical perspective.

HISTORICAL ASPECTS

The modern game of tennis bears little resemblance to the game which was played in ancient Greece and which supposedly is its historical ancestor. At best, it can be said that games in which a ball was hit against a wall, and later back and forth between two persons, were played as early as the 1400s. The boundaries, the shape of the court, and the equipment are little related to their modern counterparts. What is important is that historical records do disclose the Grecian game *sphairistike* and the "court tennis," or "racquets," of the 1870s as the forerunners of today's game of lawn tennis.

Regardless of whether or not he was the actual inventor of lawn tennis, Major Clopton Wingfield is credited with introducing tennis in 1873 in England. Mary Outerbridge, in turn, introduced it to the United States in 1875.

Of special interest are these dates:

1881 The United States Lawn Tennis Association was organized. It is now known as the USTA.

The first national championships in the United States were held in men's singles and doubles.

1887 The first national championships in the United States were held in women's singles.

1890 The first national championships in the United States were held in women's doubles.

1900 The Davis Cup international competition between men was inaugurated. The cup was donated by Dwight F. Davis, U.S.A.

1923 The Wightman Cup competition between women from England and the United States was inaugurated. The cup was donated by Hazel H. Wightman, U.S.A.

1963 The International Lawn Tennis Federation inaugurated the Federation Cup. The competition is open to women's teams from various countries, and the competitive rules are patterned after those for the Davis Cup except that teams from each country meet at a single site and only two singles and one doubles match is played by each team.

1968 The beginning of Open Tennis. The first time in the history of the sport that amateurs and professionals competed in the same tournament.

1969 The Grand Prix for Men and Women competition sponsored by the ILTF and the USTA. Open to amateurs, professionals, and independent professionals (not under contract to a specific tour group). Points are awarded on the basis of how well they finish in each tournament. The winner in overall point standings gets a money prize in addition to the amount won in an individual tournament.

1970 The Virginia Slims Circuit for Women competition for women professionals. Prize money awarded. The first women's pro tour.

World Championship Tennis is a group of professionals who are under contract to one organization to play a designated number of tournaments exclusive of competitors not under WCT contract.

1972 The Belle Cup the newest competition in tennis. Women players from United States and Australia compete against each other.

1975 World Team Tennis. A tennis-team league set up like other professional sports in that various cities buy team franchises, draft team players (men and women), have playoffs to determine the number-one team, name all-star teams, and sponsor all-star competitions.

The scoring is confusing to the spectators at their first match. The following example explains the system.

	Team 1	Team 2
MS	6	3
WS	5	7
M Dbls	6	2
W Dbls	4	6
Mxd Dbls	4	6
	25	24

Team No. 1 is the winner since they won one more game than Team No. 2. In the event of a tie there is a sudden-death playoff involving the mixed-doubles team. Each player can participate in only two events, e.g., women's singles and women's doubles. The most difficult adjustment in the team-tennis concept has been the conduct of players and fans. The loud yelling — at times supportive, at other times booing — is encouraged! This means professional tennis has "come a long way, baby!"

1979 Avon Professional Circuit for Women. Avon replaced Virginia Slims as sponsor of the women's tour.

These dates are not the only ones which are significant in the history of tennis. There are individual days and certain years, and even particular decades, which bring to mind a flood of memories to tennis enthusiasts all over the world, both spectators and participants.

Historical records are not complete without mention of people and their significant accomplishments. Tennis history is no exception. Records, preserved by the United States Tennis Association,[1] carry a complete list of champions since 1881.

GREAT ACHIEVEMENTS

Tennis is one of the world's fastest-growing sports for both participants and spectators. Television and newspaper coverage have accompanied this popular growth. To be able to recognize names and events is an added enjoyment for the beginning player.

To tennis players just starting to play in the 1980s, the names of these leading male players should become part of any conversation about tennis: Ken "Muscles" Rosewall, Rod "The Rocket" Laver and John Newcombe, Australia; Stan Smith, Arthur Ashe, Cliff Richey, Bob Lutz and Marty Riessen, U.S.A.; Zeljko Franulovic, Yugoslavia; Jan Kodes, Czechoslovakia; Illie Nastase, Romania; and Tom Okker, Netherlands. These players dominated the men's tennis world from the 1960s until recently. However, during the past three or four years, and since they are younger, the following new men stars are currently "winning it all": Jimmy Connors, Vitas Gerulaitis, Dick Stockton, Harold Solomon, Eddie Dibbs, Roscoe Tanner, Brian Gottfried and Sherwood Stewart and Fred McNair (doubles only), U.S.A.; John Alexander, Phil Dent and Colin Dibley, Australia; Andriano Pinatta and Corrado Barazzutti, Italy; Manuel Orantes, Spain; Bjorn Borg, Sweden; Guillermo Vilas, Argentina; and Raul Ramirez, Mexico. In addition to winning the prestigious rankings, they are winning prize money of up to $100,000 per final event and even more in "head-on" winner-take-all television events. Can you imagine winning over $800,000 in one year for "just playing tennis"? (No specific mention is made of the many outstanding collegiate stars, mainly because they usually move quickly into the professional ranks.)

The leading women players in the world include Evonne Goolagong Cawley, Kerry Melville Reid and Margaret Court, Australia; Nancy Richey Gunter, Billy Jean King, Chris Evert and Rosemary Casals, U.S.A.;

[1]United States Tennis Association, 120 Broadway, New York, NY

Francoise Durr, France; and Virginia Wade and Ann Haydon Jones, England.

Many of these stars — specifically Francoise Durr, Billy Jean King, Rosie Casals, Evonne Goolagong Cawley, Kerry Melville Reid and Virginia Wade — are still listed prominently among the top winners along with more recent women players. However, Chris Evert Lloyd — everyone's "Ideal American Girl" and tennis's first millionairess (1977)—has dominated the major titles, rankings, and money winnings since 1974. She is merely beginning to rewrite the record book, and has been joined by newcomers Dianne Fromholtz and Wendy Turnbull, Australia; Betty Stove, The Netherlands; Virginia Ruzici, Romania; Martina Navratilova, who defected from Czechoslavakia and is now living in the United States; and Sue Barker, England. This new talent will undoubtedly keep the spectators from being bored for some time. And such already-proven newcomers as 16-year-olds Tracy Austin and Pam Shriver, and 19-year-old John McEnroe have captured the hearts of tennis enthusiasts the world over and are clearly among the rising stars to watch.

This list is by no means conclusive, and no doubt additions will be added as players retire and youngsters develop.

The mention of current stars and recalling players of earlier eras will give the new tennis player a sense of admiration for the herculean feats of selected players since the beginning of tennis. These champions are firmly implanted in the minds of tennis players throughout the world.

In the United States Open from 1940 to 1972 Pauline Betz, Margaret Osborne du Pont, Maureen Connolly, Margaret Smith Court, Maria Bueno and Billy Jean King, won three or four women's singles titles to distinguish themselves. Since 1975 Chris Evert Lloyd has won the title four times. Other distinguished players are Doris Hart, Shirley Fry Irwin, Darline Hard, Althea Gibson and Evonne Goolagong Cawley. Even though no male player was able to accomplish a string of two or more singles titles since 1930, nonetheless the names of these champions stand out: Ellsworth Vines, Fred Perry, Don Budge, Frank Parker, Jack Kramer, Pancho Gonzales, Rodney

Laver, Ken Rosewall, Roy Emerson, John Newcombe, Stan Smith, and Jimmy Connors.

Year	Champion	Event	Tournament
1881-1887	R. D. Sears	MS*	USTA Championship
1907-1911	W. A. Larned	MS	USTA Championship
1920-1925, 1929	Wm. T. Tilden	MS	USTA Championship
1882-1887	R. D. Sears– J. Dwight (5) S. Clark (1)	MDbls*	USTA Championship
1907-1910	Fred Alexander– Harold Hackett	MDbls	USTA Championship
1915-1918, 1920-1922, 1926	Molla Bjurdstedt Mallory	WS*	USTA Championship
1923-1925, 1927-1929, 1931	Helen Wills	WS	USTA Championship
1932-1935	Helen Jacobs	WS	USTA Championship
1936, 1938-1940	Alice Marble	WS	USTA Championship
1975-1978	Chris Evert Lloyd	WS	USTA Championship
1942-1950, 1955-1957	Louise Brough, Margaret du Pont	WDbls*	USTA Championship
1951-1954	Shirley Fry, Doris Hart	WDbls	USTA Championship
1958-1962	Darlene Hard (three different partners: Maria Bueno, Jeanne Arth, and Lesley Turner)	WDbls	USTA Championship
1943-1946	Margaret du Pont– Bill Talbert	MxdDbls*	USTA Championship
1950-1956	Margaret du Pont– Ken McGregor	MxdDbls	USTA Championship
	Margaret du Pont– Ken Rosewall	MxdDbls	USTA Championship
1958-1960	Margaret du Pont– Neale Fraser	MxdDbls	USTA Championship

*MS—Men's Singles   WDbls—Women's Doubles   MDbls—Men's Doubles
WS—Women's Singles   MxdDbls—Mixed Doubles

Note: For complete records of players, countries, dates, and achievements consult the Official USTA Tennis Yearbook and Guide. Only special mention of great achievements in the USTA championships are included.

Grand Slam

This remarkable feat refers to one player winning the singles title in what is considered to be the four major tournaments in the world: the Australian Championships, the Wimbledon Championships, the French Championships, and the U.S. Championships. Don Budge of the U.S.A. was the first to achieve this honor in 1937. Since that time two women, Maureen "Little Mo" Connolly, U.S.A., and Margaret Smith Court and Rod "The Rocket" Laver, Australia, have done so. Laver's feat is further distinguished in that he accomplished it twice, once as an amateur and a decade later as a professional.

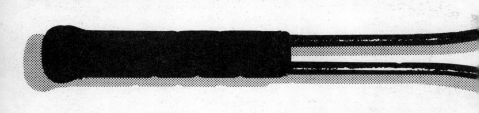

Throughout the past ninety years the number of participants in the game of tennis in the United States has increased beyond belief. The game has spread from private clubs catering to a select few to the public recreational centers open to all.

Rivalries and friendships have spiced the game, beginning with those attributed to Molla Mallory of the United States and Suzanne Lenglen of France, to that of Nancy Richey Gunter and Billy Jean King of the United States, Chris Evert Lloyd and Martina Navratilova, and Margaret Smith Court and Maria Bueno. Interestingly enough, the press documents these "rivalries" but does not become specific about men stars through the years, such as Big Bill Tilden and "the world," and Jimmy Connors and Bjorn Borg, whose rivalry recently achieved world status!

The game once played by kings now ranks as "king of games" played by millions and enjoyed by all. With the introduction of open tennis tournaments in which amateurs and professionals may compete together, a whole new era of tennis participation has opened for both players and spectators.

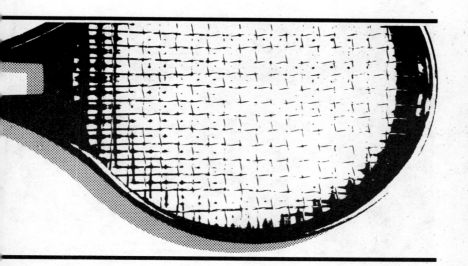

2

TALKING TENNIS

ACE
A perfect service that is not even touched by the opponent.

Ad
Abbreviation for "advantage." This occurs after a player or team has won the point immediately following deuce.

Advantage
Next point after deuce. "Advantage in" refers to the server's having won the point; "advantage out" refers to the receiver's having won the point.

All

Score is tied. This is used when deuce is not applicable, such as "30 all" or "15 all."

Alley

Area between the singles sideline and the sideline on a doubles court.

American Twist

An advanced service by which the ball is caused to spin and bounce high.

Backcourt

Area of the court between the service line and the baseline; also referred to as "no man's land."

Backhand

Stroke used to hit balls to the left side of a right-handed player and to the right side of a left-handed player.

Backspin

Rotation of the ball so that the ball spins backward.

Backswing

The act of taking a racket back to hit a ground stroke.

Ball Boy/Girl

Term referring to a person who retrieves balls for players in important matches.

Baseline

Boundary line at each end of the court.

Break a Serve

Phrase used to indicate winning a game which one's opponent has served.

Bye

A term which indicates that a player will not compete in the first round in a single elimination tournament.

Cannon Ball

A very hard flat service.

Center Mark

Mark 4″ long and 2″ wide that bisects the baseline to indicate one limit of the proper service area.

Center Service Line

Dividing line of the center of the two service courts.

Center Strap

Two-inch-wide piece of canvas that secures the net at the center of the court.

Chip

A modified slice, using little backswing.

Choke

A term usually referring to a situation in which a player misses an easy shot, becomes tense and performs poorly, or holds the racket closer to the throat than he ordinarily does.

Chop

Stroke in which the racket is drawn down sharply behind the ball to give it backspin.

Cross-Court

Refers to a ball which has been hit diagonally from one corner of the court across the net to another corner (not down the line).

Deep

Referring to a shot that lands near the baseline.

Default

Failure to appear for a scheduled match.

Deuce

Even score when each side has won three or more points.

Dink

A style in which most balls are hit — very soft, high, and sometimes in an unorthodox manner. Not able to hit an outright winner.

Double Fault

Failure to deliver ball validly on two consecutive services.

Doubles

Two persons play on each side (team).

Draw

A tournament bracket revealing the names of players and opponents.

Drive

Shot hit hard without much of an arc so that it lands near the opponent's baseline.

Drop Shot

Shot hit easily with backspin so that it barely clears the net and does not bounce very high in the opponent's court.

Error

Failure to make a legal return though racket has hit the ball.

Face

The surface of the racket used to strike the ball, or the string area.

Fault

Failure to make a legal service.

Flat

Ground stroke or service without spin.

Foot Fault

Illegal movement of the feet during service, (such as standing on line or stepping into playing court before service is completed).

Forcing Shot

Deep, hard shot designed to maneuver an opponent out of position.

Forecourt

Area of the court between the net and the service line.

Forehand

Stroke used to hit balls to the right side of a right-handed player and to the left side of a left-handed player.

Game

Unit of a set completed by winning four points before opponent wins three, or by winning two consecutive points after deuce.

Good

Shot that lands on or within the proper boundary lines.

Grip

The proper way to hold the racket; the area of the racket handle covered with leather.

Ground Stroke

Refers to a hit by either the backhand or the forehand, after the ball has bounced.

Half-Volley

Stroke made by hitting the ball immediately after it has hit the court and is on the rise.

Handle

Extension of the frame from the gripping area to the head of the racket.

Head

Part of the racket used to strike the ball; the strings and frame.

Kill or Smash

A ball that is hit before it bounces, usually overhead and in the air, which the opponent cannot reach to return.

Let

Service or point that is to be replayed because of some type of interference. (Ball touches net on service but falls into legal court — outside interference of play.)

Lob

Offensive: A shot hit with a low arc so that it lands near the opponent's baseline. Defensive: A shot hit with a high arc that enables a player to regain playing position.

Love

No score.

Long

Refers to a ball which lands outside the service line or base line following a serve or a ground stroke.

Match

Contest between two or four players, usually consisting of the best two out of three sets. Major tournaments may require best three out of five sets for men.

Match Point

Point which, if won, allows a player to win the match.

Mix-Up
Changing the pace of play; varying your shots.

Mixed Doubles
Game in which a man and a woman play as partners on each side.

Net Player
Player in doubles who plays near the net while his partner serves.

No Man's Land
Area between baseline and service line; see *backcourt*.

Open Tennis
Refers to tournaments in which both amateurs and professionals may compete.

Overhead Smash
Shot made with a hard overhead stroke so that the ball comes down sharply into the opponent's court. This shot is usually referred to as the "smash" or "kill."

Pace
The speed of the ball or the strategy employed during a match.

Passing Shot
A shot which cannot be reached by an opponent who has advanced to the net.

Placement
Shot placed to a certain area of the court or placed accurately out of reach of the opponent.

Poach
A situation in which a member of a doubles team will move over into his partner's playing area to hit a winner.

Press
To force, attack; a wooden frame fitted over the racket to prevent warping.

Rally
Continued play between the serve and the winning of a point. Also refers to pregame warm-up period.

Retrieve
Return a difficult shot.

Rush(ing)

To advance to the net; offensive style of play.

Seeding

Placing the most highly skilled performers in tournament competition in such a way as to prevent their meeting in early round play.

Service

Putting the ball into play.

Set

Unit of a match completed by one player winning six games and leading by at least two or by winning two consecutive games after each player or team has won five games, or leading by one game in a tiebreaker.

Set Point

Point which, if won, allows a player to win the set.

Singles

A match with one person on each side of the net.

Slice

Stroke in which the racket is drawn sharply down across the ball with wrist action to give sidespin.

Take the Net

Player advances to a position close to the net or forecourt to volley.

Tape

A canvas band that covers the cord or cable at the top of the net.

Throat

The area of the racket between handle and the head.

Topspin

Hitting the ball so that it spins forward or bounces high after it hits the court. The ball is hit with a flat face and upon impact the face is closed.

Toss

The spin of the racket at the beginning of a match to determine who has choice of serving or receiving; or of side of court.

Umpire
An official who keeps the score and makes line decisions during a match.

Volley
Ball hit in the air before it bounces, usually in the forecourt.

Wide
A service or ground stroke that lands beyond the side boundaries of the service court.

Woodshot
A ball which strikes the racket frame but is legal if it goes into the playing area.

IMPORTANT TEAM COMPETITIONS

Davis Cup
Competition between male teams consisting of four players each, representing their respective countries throughout the world. Four singles matches and one doubles match are played. The United States has won the cup more often than any other nation. Australia is second.

Federation Cup
International Competition between female teams consisting of at least two players, each representing their respective countries. Two singles and one doubles match are played by opposing countries. Australia has won seven times and the U.S.A. has won nine times.

Wightman Cup
Competition between female teams consisting of five players each, representing England and the United States. Five singles matches and two doubles matches are played. The United States has far outdistanced England in these matches, but the struggle has often been close.

Nations Cup
Competition between male representatives from any country in the world. Two singles matches and one doubles match are played during the single elimination.

Bonne Belle Cup

Competition between female teams from Australia and the United States. Five singles and two doubles matches are played.

Aetna World Cup

Competition between male competitors from the United States and Australia. Five singles and two doubles matches are played.

MAJOR INTERNATIONAL CHAMPIONSHIPS

USTA Open championships held at Flushing Meadows, New York. Formerly called the Forest Hills Championships; the site has changed but the name remains the same.

Wimbledon Generally accepted as the World Grass Court Championships. Held annually at Wimbledon, England.

Australian National Championships, French National Championships, German National Championships, Italian National Championships and **South African National Championships** These tournaments are referred to as the National Championships of the particular country but top-ranking players from all countries may enter.

United States National Championships (i.e., United States Amateur Grass Court Championships, Longwood Cricket Club, Boston, Mass., **National Clay Court Championships, National Indoor Championships, National Hard Court Championships**) are designated as national championships of the United States but are open to players from other countries. Additional national championships held in the United States include the **National Public Parks Championships** and the **National Intercollegiate Championships.** Participation in these two tournaments is determined by a qualification process. In the United States tournaments, other than the National Intercollegiate, tournaments have special age divisions: girls and boys under 12, singles and doubles, girls and boys over 12 and under 15, singles and doubles; and girls and boys over 15 and under 18, singles and doubles. This, of course, prevents a 12-year-old from having to compete against an 18-year-old unless a player chooses to play in an older age bracket. Upon reaching the age of 18, a player is considered to be in men's or women's divisions and there is no further categorization until age 35, which is referred to as Junior Veterans.

The major professional championships resulting from the various men's and women's pro tournament tours are:

Avon Championship The top eight women competitors from the tour play each other. (Formerly Virginia Slims.)

World Championship of Tennis Championships The top eight men competitors from the tour play each other.

Colgate Grand Prix (originally named and sponsored by Commercial Union Insurance and Pepsi). The top ten male competitors from the tour play each other.

Grand Masters A tour and championship playoff for men players, 45 and older. This event has proven quite popular with fans, since many of the past champions — for example, Torben Ulrich, Frank Sedgeman, Pancho Gonzales and Vic Seixas — prove they have a lot left. Unfortunately there is as yet no similar championship for women.

World Team Tennis (WTT) What is 78 feet long and 36 feet wide? It may be a combination of green, yellow, red, and blue squares and beige alleys. Of course it's the decorative court for World Team Tennis. Throw in the players' uniforms, at a time when individual style and color is at its height, and you have the team uniform concept.

When WTT was born in 1973, largely the brainchild of Larry and Billy Jean King, major cities supporting professional sports of all types jumped on the bandwagon. Their team names were tennis-oriented, of course — Los Angeles Strings, New York Nets, New Orleans Sets, Detroit Loves.

Attendance ranged from the umpires, players, and maintenance and refreshment personnel to crowds, five years later, of 15,000 and more.

One of the characteristics of WTT which is hard to get used to is crowd behavior. Loud yelling, booing, coaches shouting instructions from the sidelines — often during a point — brought chills and tears to those who thought of tennis as a ladies' and gentlemen's game. Times change, and this behavior has now spilled into the stands at Wimbledon and the U.S. Open.

WTT is firmly embedded in the pro-sports family, and one need only experience the super tie breaker (described on page 36) to get caught up in the true team spirit of what was originally an individual sport.

3

EQUIPMENT AND FACILITIES

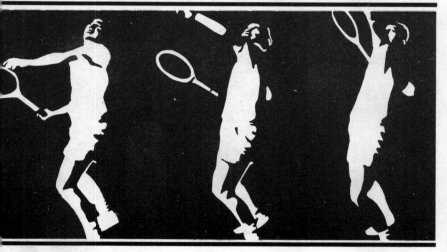

PLAYING APPAREL

The wearing of proper tennis attire is a tradition of long standing. Until Gussy Moran walked onto the courts at Wimbledon with a touch of gold lamé occasionally showing from beneath her tennis dress, all white was a requirement. The first consideration concerning color of one's attire depends upon the rules of the particular club or area where one is to play.

Many tournaments require their entrants to wear all white. Some private clubs permit colored accessories. Generally speaking, if you always want to be dressed in excellent tennis taste, stick rather closely to the rules of club, tournament, or team to avoid controversy.

In an attempt to promote spectator participation at professional matches participants often wore a variety of different-colored uniforms, i.e., yellow, blue, red. If your section or ticket stub matched a player's attire, you were to applaud for that player. This procedure did not produce the intended results, but professional players still appear in various colors for match play.

Men. For casual play, men usually will select a cotton T-shirt, shorts, tennis sneakers, snug-fitting cotton socks, and a warm-up jacket or sweater. One need not buy well-known brands of tennis clothes to be correct.

Figure 3.1 *Playing apparel.*

Shirts with collars may be added for special occasions. Figure 3.1 shows a variety of casual tennis attire for both men and women.

Women. Women usually pay more attention to their style than do most men. Even though a neat knit or cotton shirt or blouse and shorts are highly acceptable, most women prefer to wear the tennis skirt or tennis dress.

Add to these pieces of apparel a tennis hat or sun shade, and a wrist band to help keep perspiration off of your grip, and you are suited out for a good game of tennis.

Putting Yourself in Your Shoes

Shoes play as large a part in winning or losing as your racket and string, and certainly more than your clothing. Deciding which type of shoe to wear can be perplexing, so let's take a look at a variety of playing conditions and court surfaces and design some "ideal" shoes.

The most common tennis surface in the United States is the hard court. Generally, hard courts play fast, become extremely hot on warm days, and tend to be slippery. There are exceptions, depending on the construction, but these characteristics generally apply. Hard courts tend to be hard on shoes and legs, and they demand good footwork — quick turns, fast stops, and sure starts. Taking all this into account, here is how I would design a shoe for those conditions.

First, the tread pattern should be a proven one in terms of absolute traction. The traditional deck sole is fine. Other patterns are good as well; however, the sole pattern is not as critical on a hard court as the type of material used to make it. On a very hard, abrasive court surface, there is a choice between a long-wearing sole or one that is easier on your legs but more prone to wear. Polyurethane soles will almost always outwear natural or synthetic rubber ones and in most cases, are far lighter; but you may pay a price for this long life in the form of sore legs or, in severe cases, shin splints. My experience with polyurethane soles has been that they seem indestructible, but on hard courts tend to tire my legs. In addition, on hot days, polyurethane soles retain heat, thus making my feet hotter. The traction of rubber-soled shoes is, in most cases, better than the urethanes, and they are cooler. In the end, it is a trade-off, and a player should decide what is most important to him. Your choice should be your own, relative to feel and fit.

What other characteristics should the ideal hard-court shoe possess? It should have a padded collar (generally urethane or leather over foam) a terry-cloth lining on a slip-resistant insole, a fairly hard fiberboard insole, and a high-backed rear for added support. The padded, coated collar prevents you from slipping forward during serves and lessens the chance of "tennis toe" and related ailments. The tongue is usually lined with a slip-resistant material for many of the same reasons. This can be terry cloth with or without padding. Most surface should have better-than-adequate ventilation, with air holes and an upper material that will "breathe."

If you are playing casual tennis on a hard surface, then your footwear needs will change. You will want long-wearing shoes with good traction, but you won't be demanding high performance. Urethane soles are a big plus here, especially if there is no excessive heat. But for sheer comfort, you might want to consider softer lining and a sole compound that may wear faster but will absorb shocks that a hard sole, such as urethane or certain types of rubber, won't.

For the comfort shoes, look to the old, established type of footwear. The lining of the shoes is usually made of tricot, which is soft and comfortable but wears fast with heavy usage. The tongue is usually lined and quite often padded.

The overall fit of these shoes emphasizes comfort and coolness, and there is certainly nothing wrong with those qualities if you are playing strictly for fun. Now, what of the upper styling and materials, and how do they relate to a shoe's performance?

There are generally two upper styles, "V-vamp" and "lace-to-toe" configurations. In today's market, the lace-to-toe models seem to be gaining wider acceptance. Generally this style has two vamps, one on each side, which lace from top to bottom with a wide toe area that does not come together. The V-vamp is more popular with women players because they have narrower feet and the style gives them a snugger, more comfortable feel. Generally, the V-vamp is tighter at the toe and in overall fit. For competition, this tends to restrict movement and the lace-to-toe shoe is more adaptable and better fitting for this style of play.

The upper materials are limited to mainly canvas and leather. Your preference here is really the only criterion to be considered. Leather is said to provide the better fit (Cangoran is an artificial material resembling kangaroo leather), while canvas is supposed to "breathe" better and be a bit lighter. For my money the only characteristic that is noticeable is that leather does seem to provide a bit more support than canvas or nylon; but a light shoe is an advantage, especially during a long match.

What about clay-court tennis? I include Har-Tru, rubisco, and other clay-type materials in this category. The "top dressing" on clay court can range from red brick dust to a grainy material on Har-Tru and other clay surfaces. The loosely packed top dressing means that a player must slide a bit in moving about the court. Although comfort and performance will remain more or less consistent on this surface, traction becomes the most important characteristic.

Clay courts are generally easy on your shoes soles as far as wear goes, but the top dressing usually gets stuck between the ridges of the tread pattern, thus restricting its usefulness. A gentle tapping of your shoe during play will help this problem, but choice of a sole pattern is very important.

Ideally, you want a pattern that will offer good traction but will allow you to slide as most accomplished clay-court players do. The nub-sole pattern isn't as good here, and the deck sole tends to fill with top dressing. In addition to the tread design, other factors to be considered are the style of game you play and the performance you seek. These closely follow the criteria covered in hard-court shoe choices. Since clay courts are generally easy on your shoes, you have a greater latitude in choosing sole materials.

For the few players fortunate enough — or unfortunate enough, depending on your outlook — to play on grass, the tread design becomes paramount. I have found the traditional deck sole to be the most acceptable design for grass in terms of traction and court preservation. The nub sole is good for traction, but groundskeepers from Longwood, Forest Hills, Newport, and the other remaining grass-court clubs in the United States hate to see that type of sole pattern on their beloved grass courts. Foot support becomes important if you are going to play competitively. For hard courts, models and styles that provide you with excellent support are suggested. (Bud Collins delights in playing barefoot on grass, but have you ever tried to clean grass stains from under your toenails?)

What should you expect to pay for a quality pair of tennis shoes? The answer depends largely on the upper materials: a good canvas shoe runs from $15 to $20; leather models range from a low of $22 to a top of $40 for the Tretorn, but most of the good ones cost between $28 and $32. Nylon uppers are sold for $23, and the new Cangoran shoes are cheaper than leather but more expensive than canvas at $26 to $30.

The prices of different models are pretty uniform wherever you buy them, but watch for sales at sporting-goods stores and pro shops. Otherwise look to resoling for your discounts. Tred 2 is the best, most established and most reputable of these resoling outfits. They do a fine job refurbishing any shoe without a molded sole for between $11 and $15.

Constructing the ideal tennis shoe is a bit like trying to design the ultimate tennis racket. There isn't such a thing. Before you decide that your old shoe is the only one you will ever wear, give some of the new models a try. Tennis shoes have come a long way from the original spikes worn on the English lawns a century ago, and there have been many improvements in the past ten years. Be realistic in evaluating your level and style of play, try on as many as possible, then make your decision.[1]

BALLS

There are several brands of tennis balls. The United States Tennis Association publishes a list of those accepted as of good quality. Quality balls usually come in pressurized cans. Balls which do not bounce very high are referred to as "dead balls." Balls which have had all the fuzz worn off them are very light and are difficult to control. The beginner should try to use new or fairly new balls each time he plays to assure good bounces. At one time all tennis balls were white. Now they may be obtained in an array of colors. The coloring has been added for night play under certain types of lighting, for identification, and for visibility. Heavy-duty balls are covered with more felt or fuzz and are supposed to last longer.

[1]Adapted from an article by Steve Fiott, "Putting Yourself in Your Shoes." *World Tennis*, October, 1977, pp. 48-50.

RACKETS

Purchase and Care of the Racket

A beginner should always secure the assistance of a professional when he selects his first racket. He should make certain that it is not too heavy and that the grip is large enough, but not so large that he cannot grasp the racket firmly. It is not necessary to buy the most expensive frame or have the racket strung with the most expensive strings while learning to play. A medium-priced racket and strings are quite serviceable until the player becomes more skillful. A press which prevents the racket frame from warping in damp weather and a canvas type cover for the face of the racket to keep it from getting wet are essential. If the racket is strung with gut, make certain that it is stored in a dry place.

Size and Shape

There is no official rule or design to dictate the size or shape of the tennis racket. In fact, rumor has it that a man once won a tournament playing with a frying pan. Be that as it may, the length of a tennis racket, 27″, and the width across the face of the racket, 9″, are now somewhat uniform among tennis players.

However, even though the length and the width (except in the Prince model) are standardized, variations in the type of wood, the weight of the racket, the size of the grip, the balance (distribution of weight) of the racket, and the cost vary noticeably.

The Racket in Your Game

The year 1953 is ancient history when it comes to tennis equipment. Technological development in equipment almost coincides with the advent of open tennis in 1968 and the subsequent influx of players and money. Manufacturers did little to extend the state of the art in the 15 years between 1953 and 1968. The development of true "revolutionary" equipment seemed to wait for the masses of tennis players who would and could afford to buy it.

From 1953 to 1968, equipment manufacturers tried to improve upon existing products. Research and development weren't the key words, as in today's market; it was more like status quo. In 1953, racket frames were almost exclusively of wood laminate construction; they still were in 1967. Wood frames were reinforced with wood and vulcanized fiber laminations and overlays in the head, throat, shoulders, and shaft. Leather grips were improved, becoming slightly thicker and more tacky for a better grip.

Aluminum now ranks second only to wood in terms of public acceptance for tennis rackets, and most major companies have a high-performance aluminum frame in their lines. (See Figure 3.2.)

Another space-age material, graphite, became a magic word, and companies began to experiment with it

Figure 3.2 *Types of rackets: steel and wood frames.*

in tennis rackets. A graphite-wood composite in late 1974 or early '75 was developed. There is no such thing as an all-graphite racket. Graphite is a drawn carbon fiber that is strong, light, and stiff. The fiber is very useful in controlling the flex of a racket, as well as its durability, but the graphite fiber must be placed in a matrix, a material that keeps fibers in line.

Wood has always been the staple of the racket industry, and even today, with all the technological advances, wood continues to lead all other types of rackets in sales volume. But wood rackets are changing, and the days of the advanced wood-based composites are upon us. In 1978 a model composed of wood, graphite, and fiberglass was introduced to test the public response.

Today, most serious competitors in the tennis market are moving to a composite line. The market seems headed to the more durable and performance composites, even though prices are higher.

Racket technology today is light years ahead of where it was in 1968, and it shows signs of continuing development, but there will never be an "ultimate" racket. We all have our individual preferences, and this will keep companies searching to provide us with that elusive "perfect" racket.[2]

Racket Strings

One of the great mysteries for most players has to do with the stuff with which rackets are strung. Is gut the badge of a "good" player or a person with money to throw away?

Many players (I include myself) feel they don't get the same touch or control with nylon as with gut. Others say there is no noticeable difference between the two. As with most tennis equipment, personal preference should always play a large role in the ultimate choice, but there are specific factors every player should consider.

Natural gut string is made from lamb or beef intestine. I would say that 99 out of 100 players — pros included — can't tell one from the other in a play test. Sheep intestine is not as heavy or thick as that of a cow, and this could make lamb's gut more resilient, but the compromise is at the expense of durability. Since each maker of natural gut string varies the manufacturing process, all brands are slightly different, which could account for variations in durability and playing characteristics.

I have found that adding color to natural gut seems to weaken the string. The blue spiral so popular in many of today's brands is a dyed strip of gut in most cases. It is then twisted in with the natural colored fibers. I have

[2]Adapted from an article by Steve Fiott, "Whys and Wherefores of the Racket Revolution." World Tennis, June, 1978, pp. 93-100.

noticed this dyed strip will, in many cases, fray long before the main string. (This is not to make a value judgment on spiral versus natural-colored gut, only to pass along personal experience.)

Today, we also have a choice between smooth and rough-textured gut. The rough gut feels almost lumpy when you run your fingers along it. If you use a micrometer to measure the diameter of the string, you will find that rough gut has variations that almost transcend the tolerances between gauges.[3]

At least the old reference of "cat gut" strings should be dispelled.

If you live in a climate with high humidity levels you

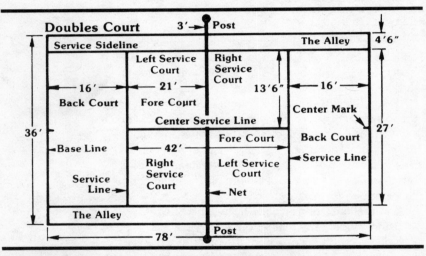

Figure 3.3 Diagrams and dimensions of tennis courts.

should keep the racket in a dry storage space to help keep the strings from going "dead."

Nylon strings are cheaper than gut. All prices range from $6.00 to $30.00 plus. Your more economical beginner rackets are already strung when purchased. Therefore you do not get a chance to select the poundage (how tight) you wish to have your strings strung by the professional. Most highly skilled players string their rackets about 55 pounds; Bjorn Borg goes as

[3]Adapted from an article by Steve Fiott, "Strings." *World Tennis,* October, 1978. pp. 44-47.

high as 80 pounds. The higher the poundage, the greater the need for control.

THE COURT

While the dimensions of the playing court for singles and doubles are rigidly set by the governing body of international tennis (see Figure 3.3), there are no restrictions placed upon the type of surface. Among the types of court surfaces are cement, clay, asphalt, grass, wood, a type of linoleum, astroturf, cork and a variety of other compositions for indoor play. The type of court surface does affect the bounce of the ball and sometimes influences the style of play developed. A hard, smooth

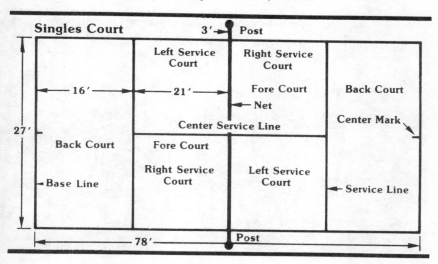

surface such as cement is a good playing surface for beginners. However, this is not necessary, and skilled players develop on courts of all types.

The Tennis Net

Most courts are equipped with a tennis net, but upon occasion one may have to provide his own net. A lightweight cotton net is available at an economical price. Tennis nets are usually made of a very durable cotton cord and are black or green. However, some playing areas furnish the wire or metal-type nets because they are permanent and more durable.

4

TENNIS RULES

Every sport is governed by a particular set of rules. The International Lawn Tennis Federation and the United States Tennis Association, ILTF and USTA, establish the rules for play internationally and in the United States. The rules for tennis are given here as they appear in the Official Tennis Umpire's Guide Book.[1]

WHAT'S THE SCORE?

Scoring in tennis has undergone serious scrutiny in

[1]Permission to reprint was graciously extended by the United States Tennis Association, and rules appear as printed in the Umpires' Manual, which they publish.

the past five years. Although several attempts have been made to improve on the traditional system, none has been successful. The game of tennis is composed of points in a game, games in a set, and sets in a match.

Scoring in a Game   (Rule 24)

Remember always to call the server's score first and practice doing so verbally:

"Love"— No Score.   "30"— Second point.

"15"— First point.   "40"— Third point.

If a player or team wins four consecutive points the game is won. If the score reaches 40–40, meaning that each player or team has won three points, this is referred to as "deuce," and one player or one team must win *two* consecutive points to win a game. The first point after deuce is "advantage in" if the server wins the point and "advantage out" if the receiver wins the point. On the point after advantage, a game is completed if the player who holds the advantage wins the point; if not, the score is again deuce.

New Scoring Procedures— The Sudden-Death Tie-Breaker

There have been a variety of experiments in scoring recently, and at last a new and exciting one has been generally accepted. It is referred to as the Tie-Breaker and follows the exact rules of scoring of games sets and matches as traditionally used *except* when games reach 6-6 in each set. The Tie-Breaker rule is then involved. At this point the players play *one* more game of nine points. In order to win a player must win five of nine points.

The 9-point tie-breaker. In this tie-breaker the play is as follows:

Player A serves for two points rotating courts as usual.

Player B serves for two points rotating courts as usual.

Player A and B change ends of the court.

Player A serves for two points rotating courts as usual.

Player B serves the remaining three points.

Note: On the ninth point the receiver may choose which court he wishes to receive in.

This example is for a game that goes the entire nine points. Games of a shorter number of points simply follow the same rotation and exchange.

12- and 13-point tie-breakers. In a 12-point playoff, players can take two serves each, changing sides after the sixth point, or split the first two serves and then continue the two-serve format (this format was used by WCT in its tournament last year).

The first player to win 7 points in the series wins the set or match. If the score reaches 6-all in a playoff, players alternate serves until one player has won two consecutive points.

If a second set must be decided in a playoff, the player who served the first two points in the initial tie-breaker now will serve second in the series.

A 13-point playoff can be implemented with this system as well. In this case, player A would serve the first two points in the series and player B would serve the last three. If the score has tied 6-all, player B would serve the last point, but player A, as the receiver, would have the choice of court.

This new system is dramatic and tension-producing. It prevents a player from playing an exhausting five hour match and not being able to recuperate for the next day's match. It aids in scheduling for television coverage, and as previously mentioned, imagine a match between Borg and Connors: score 4-6, 6-4, 6-6, four points each, one point left, and $100,000 and the number one ranking hinging on one point!

The No-Add System

This system is one employed frequently in collegiate tennis matches. The points are scored as in this example:

Player A	Player B
1st point — 1	1st point — 0
2nd point — 2	2nd point — 0
3rd point — 2	3rd point — 1
4th point — 2	4th point — 2
5th point — 3	5th point — 2
6th point — 3	6th point — 3

Six points have now been played and the score is three points for both players A and B. Normally, by the traditional scoring system, the score would be deuce and the players would go to the "advantage," where one player must win two points in succession in order to win the game. The game could go on indefinitely.

However, using the "no-add" system, when either player wins the next point (7th) the game is complete, e.g., 4-3. This system makes play and completion quicker.

Scoring in a Set   (Rule 25)

In order to win a set, a player or team must win at least six games and be leading by as many as two games (e.g., 6-3 or 6-4 is one complete set; 6-5 is not, and 7-5 is a complete set) except in tournaments where the tie-breaker is used. In this case, after games become 6-6, one more game is played using the sudden death, or 12-13 point tie-breaker.

Scoring in a Match   (Rule 26)

Most official matches consist of:

1. Men's singles — Best two out of three sets unless it is a major championship such as Wimbledon, Flushing Meadows, or the Davis Cup.

2. Men's doubles — Best two out of three sets unless it is a major championship such as Wimbledon, Flushing Meadows, or the Davis Cup.

3. Ladies' singles — Best two out of three sets. Ladies' doubles — Best two out of three sets. Mixed doubles — Best two out of three sets.

TOURNAMENT PLAY

Even though you are a beginner and may never play in a big state or national tournament, you should understand the types of tournament draws which can be made.

Single Elimination. This is the most popular type of tournament. All of the names of the players are placed in a hat or box and drawn out individually. If you lose one match you are eliminated from the tournament.

Double Elimination. This type of tournament is conducted in the same manner as the single elimination except that after losing one match the loser is placed in a consolation bracket and may continue to play until he loses a second time.

Round-Robin Tournament. Refers to a tournament in which each player plays every other player and the wins and losses are tabulated.

Ladder Tournament (also referred to as a Challenge Tournament). Is conducted so that a player ranked below may challenge the player who is one or two rungs above him on the ladder. If the challenger loses he stays in his same position. If he wins he exchanges positions on the ladder with the player whom he defeated.

OFFICIAL RULES OF TENNIS

The appended Code of Rules and Cases and Decisions, revised to 1959, is the Official Code of the International Lawn Tennis Federation, of which the United States Tennis Association is a member.

The Glossary of Terms and the Tournament Regulations are addenda adopted by the United States Tennis Association and are official in the United States only, although they in no way conflict with the Code or with international practice.

Explanations, though they are not official utterances, may be considered a correct guide for interpreting the Rules. They have been prepared by the Tennis Umpires Association to amplify and explain the formal Code.

The Singles Game—Rule 1

Dimensions and Equipment. The court shall be a rectangle 78' long and 27' wide. It shall be divided across the middle by a net, suspended from a cord or metal cable of a maximum diameter of ⅓", the ends of which shall be attached to, or pass over, the tops of two posts, 3'-6" high, the center of which shall be 3' outside the court on each side. The height of the net shall be 3' at the center, where it shall be held down taut by a strap not more than 2" wide. There shall be a band covering the cord or metal cable and the top of the net not less than 2″ nor more than 2½″ in depth on each side. The lines bounding the ends and sides of the court shall respectively be called the baselines and the sidelines. On each side of the net, at a distance of 21′ from it and parallel with it, shall be drawn the service lines. The space on each side of the net between the service line and the sidelines shall be divided into two equal parts, called the service courts, by the center service line, which must be 2″ in width, drawn halfway between and parallel with the sidelines. Each baseline shall be bisected by an imaginary continuation of the center service line to a line 4″ in length and 2″ in width, called the center mark, drawn inside the court at right angles to and in contact with such baselines. All other lines shall be not less than 1″ nor more than 2″ in width, except the baseline, which may be 4″ in width, and all measurements shall be made to the outside of the lines.

Note: In the case of the International Lawn Tennis Championship (Davis Cup) or other official championships of the International Federation, there shall be a space behind each baseline of not less than 21′, and at the sides of not less than 12′.

Rule 2

Permanent Fixtures. The permanent fixtures of the court shall include not only the net, posts, cord or metal cable, strap, and band, but also, where there are any such, the back and side stops, the stands, fixed or movable seats and chairs round the court, and their occupants, all other fixtures around and above the court, and the umpire, foot-fault judge, and linesmen when in their respective places.

Note: For the purpose of this rule, the word "umpire" encompasses the umpire and all those persons designated to assist him in the conduct of a match.

Rule 3

Ball Size, Weight, and Bound. The ball shall have a uniform outer surface. If there are any seams they shall be stitchless. The ball shall be more than 2½″ and less than 2⅝″ in diameter, and more than 2 oz. and less than 2¹⁄₁₆ oz. in weight. The ball shall have a bound of more than 53″ and less than 58″ when dropped 100″ upon a concrete base, and a deformation of more than 0.265″ and less than 0.290″ when subjected to pressure of 18 lbs. applied to each end of any diameter. All tests for bound, size, and deformation shall be made in accordance with the regulations in the Appendix hereto.

Note: "How often may a player have new balls?" According to Tournament Regulation 14g, the umpire, subject to the approval of the referee, may decide when new balls are required to ensure fairness of playing conditions. In matches where there is no umpire, the players should agree beforehand on this matter.

Rule 4

Server and Receiver. The players shall stand on opposite sides of the net; the player who first delivers the ball shall be called the server and the other the receiver.

Rule 5

Choice of Sides and Service. The choice of sides and the right to be server or receiver in the first game shall be decided by toss. The player winning the toss may choose or require his opponent to choose

(a) the right to be server or receiver, in which case the other player shall choose the side; or

(b) the side, in which case the other player shall choose the right to be server or receiver.

Rule 6

Delivery of Service. The service shall be delivered in the following manner: immediately before commencing to serve, the server shall stand with both feet at rest behind (i.e., farther from the net than) the baseline, and within imaginary continuation of the center mark and sideline. The server shall then project the ball by hand into the air in any direction and before it hits the ground, strike it with his racket; the delivery shall be deemed to have been completed at the moment of the impact of the racket and the ball. A player with the use of only one arm may utilize his racket for the projection.

Rule 7

Foot Fault. The server shall throughout the delivery of the service

(a) Not change his position by walking or running.

(b) Not touch, with either foot, any area other than that behind the baseline with the imaginary extension of the center mark and sideline.

Note: The following interpretation of Rule 7 was approved by the International Federation on July 9, 1958:

(a) The server shall not, by slight movements of the feet which do not materially affect the location originally taken up by him, be deemed "to change his position by walking or running."

(b) The word "foot" means the extremity of the leg below the ankle.

Rule 8

From Alternate Courts.

(a) In delivering the service, the server shall stand alternately behind the right and left courts, beginning from the right in every game. If service from a wrong half of the court occurs and is undetected, all play resulting from such wrong service or services shall stand, but the inaccuracy of the station shall be corrected immediately, when it is discovered.

(b) The ball served shall pass over the net and hit the ground within the service court which is diagonally opposite, or upon any line bounding such court, before the receiver returns it.

Explanation of Rule 8. In the absence of a linesman and umpire, it is customary for the receiver to determine whether the service is good or not.

Rule 9

Faults. The service is a fault

(a) if the server commits any breach of Rules 6, 7, or 8;

(b) if he misses the ball in attempting to strike it;

(c) if the ball served touches a permanent fixture (other than the net, straps, or band) before it hits the ground.

Rule 10

Service After a Fault. After a fault (if it be the first fault), the server shall serve again from behind the same half of the court from which he served that fault, unless the service was from the wrong half, when, in accordance with Rule 8, the server shall be entitled to one service only from behind the other half. A fault may not be claimed after the next service has been delivered.

Rule 11

Receiver Must Be Ready. The server shall not serve until the receiver is ready. If the latter attempts to return the service, he shall be deemed ready. If, however, the receiver signifies that he is not ready, he may not claim a fault because the ball does not hit the ground within the limits fixed for the service.

Explanation of Rule 11. The server must wait until the receiver is ready for the second service as well as the first, and if the receiver claims to be not ready and does not make any effort to return a service, the server may not claim the point, even though the service was good.

Rule 12

A Let. In all cases where a let has to be called under the rules, or to provide for an interruption to play, it shall have the following interpretation:

(a) When called solely in respect of a service, that one service only shall be replayed.

(b) When called under any other circumstances, point shall be replayed.

Rule 13

The service is a let

(a) If the ball served touches the net, strap, or band, and is otherwise good, or, after touching the net, strap, or band, touches the receiver or anything which he wears or carries before hitting the ground.

(b) If a service or a fault be delivered when the receiver is not ready (see Rule 11). In case of a let, that particular service shall not count, and the server shall serve again, but a service let does not annul a previous fault.

Rule 14

When Receiver Becomes Server. At the end of the first game the receiver shall become server, and the server receiver, and so on alternately in all the subsequent games of a match. If a player serves out of turn, the player who ought to have served shall serve as soon as the mistake is discovered, but all points scored before such discovery shall be reckoned. If a game shall have been completed before such discovery, the order of service remains as altered. A fault served before such discovery shall not be reckoned.

Rule 15

Ball in Play till Point Decided. A ball is in play from the moment at which it is delivered in service. Unless a fault or a let be called, it remains in play until the point is decided.

Rule 16

Server Wins Point. The server wins the point

(a) if the ball served, not being a let under Rule 13, touches the receiver or anything which he wears or carries before it hits the ground;

(b) if the receiver otherwise loses the point as provided by Rule 18.

Rule 17

Receiver Wins Point. The receiver wins the point

(a) if the server serves two consecutive faults;

(b) if the server otherwise loses the point as provided by Rule 18.

Rule 18

Where Player Loses Point. A player loses the point if

(a) he fails, before the ball in play has hit the ground twice consecutively, to return it directly over the net (except as provided in Rule 22a or 22c); or

(b) he returns the ball in play so that it hits the ground, a permanent fixture, or other object outside any of the lines which bound his opponent's court (except as provided in Rule 22a and 22c); or

(c) he volleys the ball and fails to make a good return even when standing outside the court; or

(d) he touches or strikes the ball in play with his racket more than once in making a stroke; or

(e) he or his racket (in his hand or otherwise) or anything which he wears or carries touches the net, posts, cord or metal cable, strap, or band, or the ground within his opponent's court at any time while the ball is in play; or

(f) he volleys the ball before it has passed the net; or

(g) the ball in play touches him or anything that he wears or carries except his racket in his hand or hands; or

(h) he throws his racket at and hits the ball.

Rule 19

Player Hinders Opponent. If a player commits any act either deliberate or involuntary which, in the opinion of the umpire, hinders his opponent in making a stroke, the umpire shall in the first case award the point to the opponent, and in the second case order the point to be replayed.

Rule 20

Ball Falling on Line—Good. A ball falling on a line is regarded as falling in the court bounded by that line.

Rule 21

Ball Touching Permanent Fixtures. If the ball in play touches a permanent fixture (other than the net, post, cord or metal cable, strap, or band) after it has hit the ground, the player who struck it wins the point; if before it hits the ground, his opponent wins the point.

Rule 22

Good Return. It is a good return

(a) if the ball touches the net, posts, cord or metal cable, strap, or band, provided that it passes over any of them and hits the ground within the court; or

(b) if the ball, served or returned, hit the ground within the proper court and rebound or be blown back over the net, and the player whose turn it is to strike reach over the net and play the ball, provided that neither he nor any part of his clothes or racket touch the net, posts, cord or metal cable, strap, or band or the ground within his opponent's court, and that the stroke be otherwise good; or

(c) if the ball be returned outside the post, either above or below the level of the top of the net, even though it touch the post, provided that it hits the ground within the proper court; or

(d) if a player's racket pass over the net after he has returned the ball, provided the ball pass over the net before being played and be properly returned; or

(e) if a player succeeded in returning the ball, served or in play, which strikes a ball lying in the court.

Rule 23

Interference. In case a player is hindered in making a stroke by anything not within his control, except a permanent fixture of the court or except as provided for in Rule 19, the point shall be replayed. For rules 24, 25, and 26, see pages 36–38.

Rule 26

When Players Change Sides. The players shall change sides at the end of the first, third, and every subsequent alternate game of each set, and at the end of each set, unless the total number of games in such set be even, in which case the change is not made until the end of the first game of the next set.

Rule 28

Rules Apply to Both Sexes. Except where otherwise stated, every reference in these rules to the masculine includes the feminine gender.

Rule 29

Decisions of Umpire and Referee. In matches where an umpire is appointed, his decision shall be final; but where a referee is appointed, an appeal shall lie to him from the decision of an umpire on a question of law, and in all such cases the decision of the referee shall be final.

The referee, in his discretion, may at any time postpone a match on account of darkness or the condition of the ground or the weather. In any case of postponement the previous score and the previous occupancy of courts shall hold good, unless the referee and the players unanimously agree otherwise.

Rule 30

Play shall be continuous from the first service till the match be concluded; provided that after the third set or, when women take part, the second set, either player is entitled to a rest, which shall not exceed 10 minutes, or in countries situated between latitude 15° north and latitude 15° south, 45 minutes, and provided further that when necessitated by circumstances not within the control of the players, the umpire may suspend play for such a period as he may consider necessary. If play be suspended and be not resumed until a later day the rest may be taken only after the third set (or when women take part, the second set) of play on such later day, completion of an unfinished set being counted as one set. These provisions shall be strictly construed, and play shall never be suspended, delayed, or interfered with for the purpose of enabling a player to recover his strength or his wind, or to receive instruction or advice. The umpire shall be the sole judge of such suspension, delay, or interference, and after giving due warning he may disqualify the offender.

The Doubles Game — Rule 31

The above Rules shall apply to the doubles game except as below.

Rule 32

Dimensions of Court. For the doubles game, the court shall be 36' in width, i.e., 4½' wider on each side than the court for the singles game, and those portions of the singles sidelines which lie between the two service lines shall be called the service sidelines. In other respects, the court shall be similar to that described in Rule 1, but the portions of the singles sidelines between the baseline and the service line on each side of the net may be omitted if desired.

Rule 33

Order of Service. The order of serving shall be decided at the beginning of each set as follows: the pair who have to serve in the first game of each set shall decide which partner shall do so and the opposing pair shall decide similarly for the second game. The partner of the player who served in the first game shall serve in the third; the partner of the player who served in the second game shall serve in the fourth, and so on in the same order in all subsequent games of a set.

Rule 34

Order of Receiving. The order of receiving the service shall be decided at the beginning of each set as follows: the pair who have to receive the service in the first game shall decide which partner shall receive in the first service, and that partner shall continue to receive the first service in every odd game throughout that set. The opposing pair shall likewise decide which partner shall receive the first service in every even game throughout the set. Partners shall receive the service alternately throughout the game.

Explanation of Rule 34. The receiving formation of a doubles team may not be changed during a set, but only at the start of a new set. Partners must receive throughout each set on the same sides of the court which they originally select when the set begins. The first server is not required to receive in the right court; he may select either side, but must hold this to the end of the set.

Rule 35

Service Out of Turn. If a partner serves out of his turn, the partner who ought to have served shall serve as soon as the mistake is discovered, but all points scored, and any fault served before such discovery, shall be reckoned. If a game shall have been completed before such discovery, the order of service remains as altered.

Rule 36

Error in Order of Receiving. If during a game the order of receiving the service is changed by the receivers it shall remain as altered until the end of the game in which the mistake is discovered, but the partners shall resume their original order of receiving in the next game of that set in which they are receivers of the service.

Rule 37

Ball Touching Server's Partner Is a Fault. The service is a fault as provided for by Rule 9, or if the ball served touches the server's partner or anything he wears or carries; but if the ball served touches the partner of the receiver or anything which he wears or carries not being a let under Rule 13a, before it hits the ground, the server wins the point.

Rule 38

Ball Struck Alternately. The ball shall be struck alternately by either player of the opposing pairs, and if a player touches the ball with his racket in contravention of this rule, his opponents win the point.

5

FUNDAMENTAL STROKES

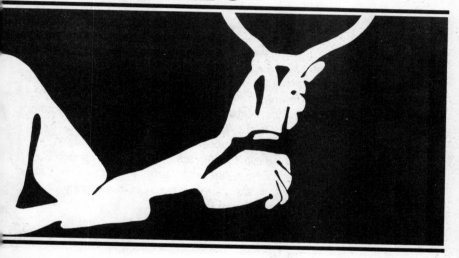

THEORETICAL OVERVIEW

So you want to learn to play tennis? There are certain priorities involved in the process of learning any motor skill. Once you have these priorities clearly identified, your progress made can be readily appraised.

A beginning tennis player may fall into one of the several skill categories. He may never have touched a racket or attempted to hit a tennis ball. He may have picked up the racket at the invitation of a friend, with little regard as to the correct grip, playing position, or stroke process, and played. Or he may have had rudimentary assistance in grip selection, but no formal assistance in grip adjustment, footwork, playing position, strategy, and other theoretical considerations which accompany the acquisition of a motor skill.

Regardless of the category in which you place yourself, each of the aforementioned categories qualifies you as a tennis beginner. Basic to the process of learning to play tennis is the *desire to learn* and an understanding of the purpose or the *why* of playing tennis. Variables which will affect your progress include physical development, strength and coordination, previous experience in physical education, self-expectation, and the amount of time you are willing to spend practicing a specific skill, not just simply playing the game.

THE ACQUISITION OF A MOTOR SKILL

Several ways in which students learn to perform a motor skill are applicable to the game of tennis. The *demonstration* or *visual* method is commonly employed in beginning tennis. This may include demonstration of correct grips, playing stance, playing positions, footwork, backswing, and follow-through of all the strokes to be learned. These demonstrations may be provided by a teacher or a top-ranking tennis player, or through the use of visual aids. Although *verbal* instruction should be minimized, it offers another popular medium by which beginners may learn to play tennis.

Manual guidance is a method by which a teacher or friend actually helps the learner by guiding him through a particular stroke at a slower speed than that with which the skill is usually performed. In a case of particular difficulty in learning a certain skill or all skills, manual guidance is suggested. It should be remembered that this method cannot substitute for performance initiated by the learner, and as quickly as he can, the learner should attempt to perform the skill individually and at the normal pace.

Practice with Purpose

You are the teacher! Even though professional guidance is usually available, essentially, you are your own best teacher. The basic factor which precedes optimum learning is, as previously mentioned, the *desire* to learn. You must set the goal or level of skill which you wish to attain and, from this beginning, *practice with purpose.*

Numerous variables affect the learning of a new motor skill. However, assuming that factors such as difficulty of the learning task, age and maturity of the average learner, and the level of skill desired are relatively equal, some general statements concerning practice schedules for a beginner may be made. When learning a new skill in tennis:

1. Practice methods should be long enough to provide some feeling of accomplishment.

2. The practice periods should be lengthened as new skills are introduced in order to provide time for the practice of the skills previously learned, as well as time to become acquainted with the new skills and time for the combining of the skills into a meaningful pattern.

3. Careful attention should be given to the number of days between practice sessions. Backsliding usually occurs when the periods of practice are too short or more than two days elapse between practice.

4. The skill should be performed correctly. Practice per se does not make perfect, but practicing perfectly or correctly the skill to be learned makes or leads to perfection of the skill.

Now that guidelines for organizing your practice schedule have been established and after selecting the basic skills to be learned, in this case the service, the forehand, and the backhand drive, you will want to consider some general statements concerning practice or rally sessions. Assuming that you wish to learn to play well enough to compete or play a good game against a friend, classmate, member of your family, club member, or even in a tournament, you should realize early that practice sessions should contribute to the formation of the physical, emotional, and mental habits of active play. Suggestions for a good practice session include:

1. Always approach a practice session eager to improve what you already can do.

2. Warm up physically with some applicable calisthenics or running prior to hitting the ball.

3. Pay careful attention to correct grips, playing stance and position, footwork, backswing, ball contact, and follow-through.

4. Hit the shots at the pace and in the manner (direction) in which they are to be hit during a regular game.

5. Practice all facets of your newly learned skills, e.g., this means execution of a forehand drive as well as the return of a service to your forehand.

6. Practice as you want to play, and do your best at all times.

In summary, it is important for the beginning tennis player to understand fully that when learning any motor skill there is constant communication between the brain, or nervous system, and the muscular system of the body. This factor indicates that learning to play tennis is a combined mental and physical process and that noticeable improvement is effected if neither is overlooked. Further, the learner must have the desire to set aside an adequate number of hours for practice sessions, must understand the involvements in each skill to be learned, and must spend a tremendous amount of hours practicing.

SELECTION OF SKILLS TO BE LEARNED

Since it is estimated that 90 percent of all shots in a tennis match are either the service, the forehand drive, or the backhand drive, these three skills have been selected as essential for the beginning tennis player. The service and the forehand and backhand drives should be emphasized before the volley because many players of all levels enjoy a good game of tennis without fully mastering the volley. Additional skills — the forehand and backhand volleys, the half-volley, the lob, the overhead smash, the chop, the slice, the drop shot, and the drop volley — will be mentioned to help the beginner realize the total components of the game of tennis. In addition to the verbal directions which follow, it is suggested that you refer to the photographs for additional clarification.

Playing Position and Stance

All playing instructions apply to right-handed players and should be reversed for left-handed players.

The game of tennis involves situations when the player is considered to be on the *offense,* or in control of the rally, or on the *defense,* when his opponent is in control. Even though there are variations in the style of play and in the level of skill of the individual and of his opponent, the player's position should always be described as *ready* or *on one's toes.*

The general rules applicable in most playing situations involving beginners follow.

Figure 5.1 *Playing position.*

Figure 5.2 *Positions of the racket face during play: (from left to right) closed, flat, and open-faced.*

Figure 5.3 *The forehand grip.*

1. Whether you are receiving a service or waiting at the baseline for a shot to be returned by your opponent, face the net, with feet spread comfortably, usually shoulder width, knees slightly bent with back fairly straight and weight slightly forward, on the balls of your feet. Hold your racket in front of you (the handle should form two right angles with your stomach if you brought it in that

close to your body). Cradle the throat of the racket in your left hand. Grip the racket firmly with a forehand grip, unless you anticipate your opponent will serve or return to the backhand. (See Figures 5.1 and 5.2.)

2. When a player is waiting to receive a service he should be approximately in the center of the service court to which the server is serving. The distance from the service line will depend upon the depth of your opponent's service. Generally you should be near the baseline and, when playing against a good server, 3′ to 6′ behind it.

Figure 5.4 *The forehand drive: pivot position to follow-through.*

3. Follow the same general rules in 1 and 2 when engaged in a baseline rally except that you should return to a position 3′ to 6′ behind the center of the baseline after each shot, if most shots are being played to the baseline and your opponent is hitting deep.

There is no set rule concerning which stroke or skill in tennis is to be learned first. However, available evidence indicates that the following pattern of learning to play tennis is common and accepted.

The Forehand Drive

By definition, the forehand drive is that stroke in tennis used to contact the ball on the right side of the player's body.

The Grip. Even though there are several grips from which a beginner may choose, the Eastern grip or the "handshake" as it is often referred to, is recommended for beginners. As you progress you will no doubt make certain adjustments in order to correct a weakness or develop a strong point.

Cradle the racket at the throat in the fingers of your left hand. Slide your right hand from the face of the

Note that side has already been turned perpendicular to the net.

racket down the handle to the grip. Your palm should now be pressed firmly against the back of the grip. Close the fingers comfortably and grip the racket firmly. (See Figure 5.3.)

The Forehand Stroke. This sequence is suggested when executing a forehand stroke (see Figure 5.4):

1. Assume the *ready* or playing position.
2. Assume the correct grip on the racket.

3. From the moment your opponent has hit the ball, watch closely to determine to which side (backhand or forehand) his return is directed. As soon as you have determined that the ball is coming to your right side you must give consideration to the correct footwork, which involves the movement of the feet on the backswing, the contact with the ball, and the follow-through. In addition, watch the ball closely until it has actually made racket contact.

4. The pivot for the forehand drive is accomplished by distributing the weight on the heel of the back foot (right foot) and turning on it as well as on the ball or toe region of the front foot (left foot). Once this has

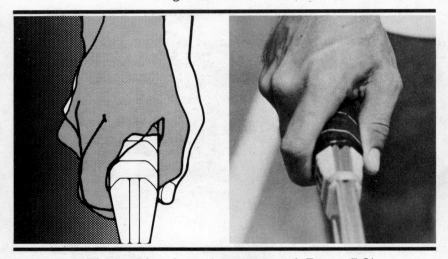

Figure 5.5 *The backhand grip (compare with Figure 5.3).*

occurred, step toward the ball with your foot and at the same time start your backswing. The backswing may start as early as when you pivot. Most of the weight is now on your back foot. At the end of the backswing the racket should be approximately at waist level, but this may vary tremendously among individuals. The important thing to remember is that at the point of contact with the ball, the racket face should be flat or slightly open and about waist level. The weight is transferred from the back foot to the front foot as the stroke is completed. A ball which bounces about waist level should be contacted at the height of its bounce with the left shoulder facing the net. A ball which bounces higher than one's head may be allowed to drop to waist level or hit with an overhead motion. Actual contact with the ball should occur well in front of your body, at a point even as far left as the left hip.

5. After the ball has been contacted, the follow-through, along with the influence of the correct foot movement, should bring the player back into a ready position facing the net. Remember to grip the racket firmly, and if you break the wrist, to do so ever so slightly. The follow-through is particularly important in that it influences the direction of the

Figure 5.6 *The backhand drive: pivoting to the left to follow-through.*

ball, the power or pace of the ball, and the way the ball bounces in your opponent's court.

The Backhand Drive

Even though the forehand drive is generally considered to be the fundamental stroke of all tennis players, the backhand drive is nonetheless essential to a sound game. By definition, the backhand drive is the stroke used to hit all balls which are to the left of the player's body. The same rules of procedure suggested for the forehand drive are applicable to the backhand drive with the exception of those which follow.

The Grip. Changing from the forehand to the backhand grip appears awkward at first but careful practice will eliminate this feeling. Grip the racket at its throat with your left hand while holding the racket with a forehand grip. Turn your right hand until the palm is on the top of the racket or the V which is formed when your thumb and index finger is to the left of the top of the grip. (See Figure 5.5.) You may choose to wrap all your fingers firmly around the grip of the racket, or you may choose to extend the thumb along the racket grip.

The Backhand Stroke. Pivoting for the execution of the backhand drive is essentially a reversal of the procedure for the execution of the forehand drive. This sequence is suggested (also see Figure 5.6):

1. Assume the ready position.

2. Cradle the racket at its throat with the left hand for added balance until the ball is approximately at the point of contact.

3. Pivot with the weight on your back (left) heel and turn on the ball or toe region of your front (right) foot. Step toward the ball with your front foot. The right shoulder should be facing the net.

4. The same principles should apply on the backswing on both the forehand and the backhand drives.

5. The ball should be contacted in front of the right hip at its height or at the peak of its bounce.

6. The follow-through and accompanying footwork should bring the player back into the correct playing position, which is facing the net.

The Service

The service is unique in that it requires the skilled coordination of both hands. It is perhaps the most essential stroke to be learned, as the service is the means by which all points are started. To the highly skilled performer or tournament player, the development of a powerful service, as well as one which involves spin or causes the ball to hop, is indispensable. To the beginner, it is only slightly less important.

The Grip. Most beginners elect to use the forehand grip for the service because the results are quicker. However, if the server desires to progress to a higher level of skill as well as develop a spin service, he should use a grip approximately halfway between the forehand and the backhand grip. (See Figure 5.7.) Some players may even elect to use the backhand grip while serving.

The Service Stroke. After the grip has been selected, assume a position 2′ or 3′ to the right of the center mark behind the baseline if you are serving to the forehand court of the opponent in singles. If you are playing doubles you may elect to move midway or

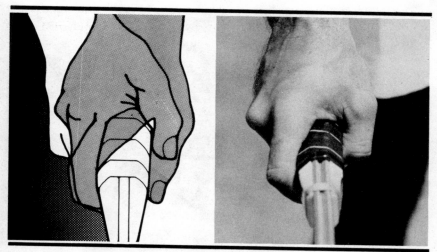

Figure 5.7 *The service grip (compare with Figures 5.3 and 5.5).*

farther from the center mark. Reverse this distance to the left of the center service line when serving to the backhand court. The feet are at an angle to the baseline.

After you have determined the grip and have taken your proper serving position on the court, time should be allotted for practicing the ball toss. Hold the ball with the thumb, the index finger, and the middle finger. The ball should be tossed as high as the racket and racket arm reach when the arm is extended.

For the flat service, the ball should be tossed in front of the shoulder of the serving arm. For the spin service, the ball should be tossed slightly more toward the left shoulder. (See Figure 5.8.)

The downward swing or backswing of the racket is started about waist level. One or two balls are held in the left hand and may be near or touching the face of the racket at the beginning of the service. Both knees are bent slightly as the weight is transferred from the back foot to the front foot. Both feet should remain in contact with the playing court to assure a firm base and to avoid possible foot faults.

On the backswing or downswing, which takes the racket behind the player's back on the service, prepare to toss the ball in the air with your left arm and hand

Figure 5.8 *The service: tossing ball to follow-through.*

extended. The elbow and the wrist of your right arm are now bent and you could actually scratch your back with the head of the racket prior to the full extension of the racket arm.

At the height of the ball toss, the racket arm should be fully extended. As the ball is contacted, the body rotates forward and the wrist is snapped at the time of contact. The follow-through is usually across the body to the left, and usually brings the right leg around where the player is facing the net or carries him across the baseline towards the net in playing position. If the beginner discovers that the grip halfway between the forehand and the backhand produces too many double faults, he should revert to the forehand grip for the service and continue to practice the other grip when not involved in actual play.

ADDITIONAL STROKES

The following discussion completes the strokes to be learned if a player wishes to continue beyond the beginning level of play.

The Volley

Some authorities declare that it is impossible to exclude the volley from the essential skills for beginners. It is recognized that the lack of the ability to volley does limit the offensive ability of the player, but many players with varying levels of skill never master the volley.

The volley may be defined as a stroke which is hit before the ball has bounced. Volleys are generally executed near the net. If the court were analogous to a clock the positions at which most volleys are hit would be 2, 3, 4, 8, 9, or 10 o-clock. In general, the opportunity to hit a volley occurs more frequently in doubles play, but the singles player who chooses an offensive plan of strategy may use the stroke often. The volley is hit from either the forehand or backhand side. The ball is contacted while still in the air.

The Grip. The grip for the volley is identical to that employed in the execution of the forehand and the backhand drives.

Court Position. When first learning to volley, the player should stand about one arm's length and one racket's length from the net, knees slightly bent, racket in front of the body, alert to hit on either side.

Meeting the Ball. If the ball is at waist level or higher, the backswing is shorter than for the drive and the face of the racket is flat or closed, depending on the height of the ball (see Figures 5.9 and 5.10). The follow-through is also shorter and the entire stroke may resemble a punch. Volleys hit below the level of the net are usually defensive shots in which the face of the racket is open in order for the ball to rise and clear the net. However, many times a soft-angled volley or drop volley is possible from this level.

The Half-Volley

This stroke is difficult to master and the success of it is contingent mainly upon your ability to time the contact of the ball immediately after it has come in contact with the court. The racket is held in a flat-face position if you are at the baseline, and in a slightly more open position the closer to the net you advance.

The Lob

The grip, stance, footwork, and backswing for the lob are similar to those used for the forehand and backhand drives. The key difference is that the face of the racket is open when you hit a lob and the racket head is much lower on the backswing, and sometimes is

Figure 5.9 *The forehand volley: note the short backswing.*
Figure 5.10 *The backhand volley: note the longer backswing.*

also lower at the point of contact. The follow-through or finish of the stroke on the lob finds the racket face slightly higher than when hitting a forehand or backhand stroke and more open. (See Figures 5.11 and 5.12.)

There are two types of lobs which may be of great use in both singles and doubles play. The offensive lob is a stroke which is concealed and barely clears the net player's head or is hit to the opponent's weakness when he is at the baseline and enables one to advance to the net. The defensive lob is a stroke used when one's opponent has hit a shot which is nearly impossible to return or when one is forced well out of the normal playing position. This shot makes a much higher arc.

The Overhead Smash

In order to play the net successfully one must master the overhead smash. This stroke resembles the service, and all principles for executing the service are generally applicable to the overhead smash. Key differences are that the player must move and get into position under the ball. There is a slight pause after the racket has been drawn back and the feet often leave the ground upon completion. (See Figure 5.13.)

Figure 5.11 *The forehand lob: note open face of racket.*

Figure 5.12 *The backhand lob: note the longer backswing than the forehand lob.*

The Drop Shot

Executing a drop shot involves essentially the same principles as the forehand and the backhand drives. However, upon touching the ball the racket imparts backspin, which slows down the forward motion. The follow-through is shorter than for the drive. The intention is to drop the ball just over the net and force the opponent to advance to the net, where he may be passed.

The Drop Volley

The drop volley involves little backswing and almost no follow-through. The face of the racket is slightly open and moves under the ball at time of contact. The grip is less tense than for other strokes.

The Chop and Slice

These two strokes are produced by eliminating most of the backswing usually necessary for the forehand and backhand drives. Chopping or slicing the ball is accomplished by cutting down and across the ball and is particularly effective on certain court surfaces; it is used to slow down or otherwise change the pace of play.

Figure 5.13 *The overhead smash: note the feet leave the ground.*

These strokes may also be used against a strong wind. The low bounce causes the opponent to hit the ball up and consequently out of bounds.

The Two-Handed Shot

In times past when teaching professionals and instructors met beginners for the first time they usually taught the fundamental one hand on the forehand and one hand on the backhand strokes.

However, when you have the top players in the world, Jimmy Connors, Bjorn Borg, Guillermo Vilas, and Chris Evert hitting two-handed shots and Frew

McMilan, the premier doubles player, hitting off both sides with two hands, notice has to be taken because TV, World Team Tennis, the Avon circuit, and the World Tennis Association circuit has given these players great publicity. Since imitation of great champions is one way of learning, two-handed shots are increasing.

The Two-Handed Forehand The preferred hand grips the racquet nearest the butt as in the ordinary one-handed forehand (Eastern-Continental). A right-handed tennis player would then place the left hand above the right on the racquet for the two-handed forehand stroke. The footwork remains the same as for the regular forehand. (See Figure 5.14.)

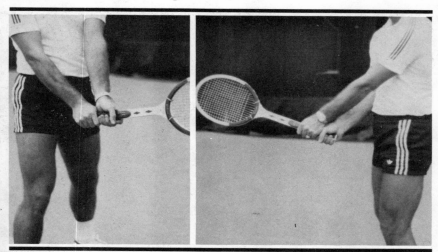

Figure 5.14 *Two handed backhand second sequence (left over right).*
Figure 5.15 *Two handed forehand for R-hand player (left over right).*

Two-Handed Backhand The preferred hand grips the racket nearest the butt as in the ordinary one-handed backhand. A right-handed player would then place the left hand above the right on the racquet. The footwork is the same as for the typical backhand. (See Figure 5.15.)

Why Two Hands? Most "two-handed players" give reasons such as: I was too small to hold the racket when I started to play; my racket grip was too large for my hand; or it just felt more comfortable or easier. There appears to be no highly researched answer at this time as to desirability. So, perhaps "to each his own" is my best response, keeping in mind that you may encounter more volley problems with two-handed than with one-handed strokes.

DIFFERENT STROKES FOR DIFFERENT FOLKS

In this chapter are outlined what could be called sound, fundamental strokes or the "ideal" way to learn tennis. However, after years as a competitor and an equal number of years as a teacher at the collegiate level, I am convinced that after beginning players have

been presented with these fundamentally sound principles they should develop skills according to their individual ability to move, their style of movement, and their choice of stroke production.

Prior to the 1970s, few if any teaching pros or physical education instructors would have advocated or permitted their beginners to hit with two hands, use an open stance, or commit any violation of the status quo attitudes toward the "right way." Today, thousands of players-to-be violate the "right way" in their search to become competent, or even tournament players. You can understand why when you look at the top-ranked players and see Evert, Austin, Connors, Borg, Vilas,

Soloman, Dibbs, and Durr defy the "right way" and play it "their way." So consider the fundamentals and then do what feels natural to you.

PLAY SMART TENNIS

You may choose to master the three basic strokes and some or all of the others. If you wish to play a satisfying game of tennis, regardless of your choice of strokes, the following suggestions bear repeating.

1. Practice correctly and often.
2. Pay careful attention to your grips, playing position, footwork, backswing, and follow-through.

3. Bend your knees.
4. Keep a firm wrist.
5. Watch the ball — hit it at the correct level of its flight.
6. Work hard on your weaknesses.
7. Remember that tennis involves a combination of mental and physical skills.

6

STRATEGY AND TECHNIQUES

ENJOYING COMPETITION

The Greeks had a marvelous attitude toward competition. They believed that one competed *with* an opponent in order to bring out the highest degree of skill possible. The element of winning or losing was still present, but in winning one should be delighted, and in losing one should be gracious. As a beginner, competition will soon be a part of your total involvement in tennis. Learn early to keep control of your emotions, and do not build up unnecessary pressures by placing too much emphasis on winning.

THE SERVICE

Characteristic of a sound game of tennis is a good service. In singles, most players prefer to hit a flat, hard service on the first ball. A great many services are directed to the right or left corner of the opponent's service court. The second service should be somewhat more conservative to avoid double faults. If you choose to hit the second service hard and flat, decrease the speed a little. A slice or twist service is a good second serve in singles. This furnishes a change of pace and assures consistency.

In doubles, the same types of service are employed, but more emphasis is placed on a high-bouncing twist service which pulls the receiver out of his normal position and enables the server to move into net position for a volley or smash.

RETURN OF SERVICE

When returning a service, it is important that you watch the ball leave your opponent's racket before making your move. A good service return is largely intuitive and involves automatic reflex actions. A player has several choices with which he can return a serve. The returns of service in singles from the forehand or backhand courts have certain basic similarities. The ready position and stance are the same but, after changing grips, the pivoting and the footwork are simply reversed. The same mechanics of backswing, contact, and follow-through are applicable. The wrist should be kept firm or locked. The basic return is a forceful forehand or backhand drive. In singles, if the opponent is a net rusher you may choose to hit the ball down-the-line, cross-court, directly at the opponent's feet, or as a well-placed lob. If the opponent remains at the baseline, a majority of the returns should be hit cross-court or near the middle of the court on the baseline. Down-the-line shots may be used for variety if the opponent has a specific weakness.

Generally speaking, when returning service from the forehand court a player should stand a foot or so behind the baseline and near the forehand alley line. The same position applies to the return from the backhand court.

However, as you observe the speed, depth, and type of bounce your opponent gives the ball, you may choose to adapt accordingly. The return of serve is not a fixed shot; if the application of sound procedures fails, experiment with your individual skill. But get the ball back into your opponent's court.

In doubles, the basic procedures for returning service are similar to those involved in singles, except that the receiver must sometimes shift his position on the baseline. The alternative returns in doubles include a sharply angled cross-court, a power drive down the middle of the court between members of the opposing team, a lob over the net player's head, a down-the-line shot when the server's partner has left his alley too soon, a hard, low shot aimed directly at the net player, or a soft chop or slice aimed at the server's feet as he advances to the net. Most shots are returned cross-court with as much power and angle as possible. The lob can be used to greater advantage in doubles. Under cover of a defensive lob, a team member can return to position. This shot usually has greater height than the offensive lob, which is generally better concealed and barely clears the opponents' heads as they play the net.

Above all, do not underestimate the importance of attention and practice on the return of service. Always remember to assume the proper ready position, get the racket back at least by the time the ball has crossed the net, and concentrate on returning the ball to your opponent's detectable weaknesses.

THE EFFECT OF COURT SURFACE

As a beginner you may not be as concerned over types of court surfaces as an advanced player, but in large metropolitan centers you no doubt will have an opportunity to play on cement, clay, asphalt, and maybe even wood or grass. The following general statements should be sufficient to aid you in adapting to either surface, or at least to prepare you for the obvious differences.

Players who have been taught on clay usually have excellent ground strokes, but often are poor volleyers because of the long rallies from the baseline and because it is more difficult to hit winning shots at the net due to the slow bounce. However, since the ball bounces so slowly on clay, power drives and smashes are more easily retrieved, and all but the highly skilled players are encouraged to hit from the baseline except in doubles. Depth, consistency, and accuracy are the most important factors when playing on clay.

On grass courts speed and flexibility are important. The ball does not bounce as high or as dependably as it does on other surfaces. Emphasis is on a shorter backswing and on the service, the volley, the smash, chops, slices, and dropshots.

On the cement, concrete, or asphalt court one has a greater choice of style of play. A player may be a baseliner, a net rusher, or a combination of these two. These surfaces are faster than clay and produce a truer, but usually higher, bounce.

A cement or grass court player adjusts to wood surfaces fairly easily. The bounce is true but somewhat faster, giving less time for the player to get set. Some wood courts are now covered with a green canvas to aid in the player's footing and vision and to slow the bounce of the ball.

Despite the ways in which court surfaces affect the bounce of the ball and style of play, if a beginner learns his fundamental strokes well he can adopt satisfactorily to most types of court surface, which now may be a combination of most anything synthetic.

BASELINE OR THE NET?

Recently there has been a great deal of controversy over whether the baseline game or the net game is the best method on which to start beginners. Inasmuch as the forehand and backhand drives are two of the essential skills for beginners, it is proposed that beginning players should concentrate on these strokes until a high degree of skill is attained. The volley should follow as a more advanced skill. In singles play, most beginners elect to rally from the baseline until drawn to the net; thus the volley should be introduced as soon as possible to enable the beginner to perform at the net when necessary in singles and in order that he may volley adequately in doubles when his partner is serving. The beginner is not usually competent enough to follow his service to the net to volley, and should usually go to the net after his opponent's return of service.

TECHNIQUES OF STRATEGY

A player's strategy is affected by his individual skill, the skill of his opponent, and the playing conditions. Generally speaking, there are two areas of the court from which a player may concentrate his play. These are referred to as the baseline or backcourt and the net or forecourt. Most beginners confine their play to the baseline in singles unless they are drawn into the net by a short-angle shot or a drop shot. In doubles, since one player is usually at the net while the partner is serving;

Figure 6.1 *The parallel position with both players at the net is the most advantageous position in doubles.*

Figure 6.2 *Return of service in singles; Y is the server.*

volleys are more common. Some sound guidelines which apply to all match play include:

1. Warm up properly, practicing all of your shots before starting the match.

2. Pay careful attention to your opponent's strengths and weaknesses during the warm-up period.

3. After the match has started, play your strengths to the opponent's weaknesses, but occasionally hit a

shot to his strong point. Usually this strategy produces an error on his part from overconfidence or from his not having hit very many shots using his strong point.

4. Never change a winning game, but always change a losing game. For example, if you are losing by hitting from the baseline, go to the net. If you are hitting your drives very hard and your opponent is handling them easily, try hitting some soft shots. If your opponent is attacking and playing the net well, lob more to the backhand side. If your serve is not proving effective, hit some slices or spin services to change the pace.

Figure 6.3 *Basic doubles formation.*

5. Against a net rusher or highly skilled volleyer, use the passing shot for power, the angled cross-court, the lob, and the soft shot, which should be aimed directly at his feet, forcing him to hit up.

6. Against a baseline player, in singles, hit most shots cross-court. The logic supporting this is that the diagonal is longer than the down-the-line shot, your opponent is moved out of position, and the ball crosses the net at its lowest point.

7. Hit down-the-line as an approach shot, as a passing shot, or when the opponent has a definite weakness.

8. Against the net rusher do not always attempt to make your first shot a winner. The skilled volleyer does not always try for a put-away on his first volley either.

Warm-Up Do's and Don'ts[1]

DON'T waste precious time by starting out hitting the ball out of your hand. DO drop the ball first, simulating a normal groundstroke.

DON'T hit down the center of the court. DO move the ball from side to side.

DON'T be oblivious to the weather conditions. DO check the angle of the sun and get a hat if necessary. DO see how the wind is blowing and how wide or deep you can hit the ball without the wind carrying it out.

DON'T slug. DO try to establish a rhythm. DO pretend each shot is the only shot you will ever hit.

DON'T hit short. DO lift the ball high over the net and deep into your opponent's court. The tenseness that will come during the match will cause you to hit shorter, so emphasize length in the warm-up and in your practice serves.

DON'T be egocentric. DO examine your opponent's strokes and offer him a variety, checking out his preferences and weaknesses.

DON'T run hot and cold. DO try to make the transition from warm-up to match as smooth as possible. Be warmed up physically and mentally by the time the match begins.

Basic Singles Strategy

If you are playing an opponent who seldom advances to the net, use the shots illustrated in Figure 6.2. In addition, it is sound strategy to employ a drop shot which forces him to advance to the net, followed by a lob if he successfully returns your drop shot.

If you are playing a net rusher, numbers 1, 2, and occasionally number 4, and a good lob are effective. If you are the net rusher your first service is generally a

[1]Tym, Alice. "From a Coach's Notebook." *World Tennis*, March, 1977, p. 35.

hard flat service to either corner; occasionally aiming
directly at the opponent's service area is effective.
The second service may be a twist resulting in a
high-bounding ball, which enables you to get in close
enough to the net to volley for a winner.

Basic Doubles Strategy

The game of doubles may produce the most
excitement and the widest variety of shots to be
experienced in tennis. The former is contingent upon the
style or formation employed by the four players
involved. The most advanced level of doubles play finds
all four players at the net position.

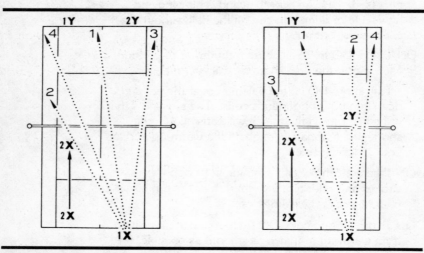

Figure 6.4a and 6.4b *Return of service in doubles; 1Y is the server.*

Figure 6.3 illustrates a sound formation of doubles
play. The shot most often used in returning service in
doubles is illustrated by numbers 1 and 3 in Figure 6.4b.
For variation, a deceptive and well-placed lob, number
2, over 2Y's head will discourage the server from
following his service to the net, or at least will force 1Y
and 2Y out of good playing position. If 2Y is poaching
or moving out of his position at the net frequently to
intercept the service return, a down-the-line shot,
number 4, will encourage him to remain in his position.

Figure 6.4a illustrates a situation frequently employed

by beginning players and women players, and sometimes as an obvious plan of strategy. Players 1Y and 2Y have elected to remain in the backcourt. In this 1X and 2X should advance to the net quickly if they have a good volley and overhead smash. Sound shots which will enable them to advance to the net include numbers 1, 2, 3, and 4.

There are many patterns of play employed in doubles. Decisions are most often based upon the level of skill of the participants, whether the match is men's, women's, or mixed doubles, and whether you are playing on a social basis or in a highly competitive situation.

The following suggestions are offered as sound guidelines for most situations in doubles play.

1. Be patient and congenial with your partner. A display of anger when your partner commits an error is poor sportsmanship and usually tends to produce more errors.

2. When both team members are at the net, a ball hit between them should usually be taken by the player who has the forehand shot or by the player who hit the last volley.

3. In good doubles play the most consistent return of service is the hard cross-court forehand or backhand, but low-dipping shots at the opponent's feet, an occasional down-the-line, and a disguised lob produce a variety of shots to keep the opponent guessing.

4. Poach only when you are almost certain you can win the point.

5. If the server remains at the baseline after serving, or if one team member is at the baseline during a rally, the player at the net should cross over and take the drop shot or short shot. This is particularly sound in mixed doubles or if the player at the baseline is slow.

6. If your opponent lobs over your head, your partner should go behind you and make the return. You should cross over into the playing area vacated by your partner.

7. In mixed doubles play, do not take more than your share of the shots or try to cover too much of the court. This tends to place both team members out of position and produces frustration and needless errors.

8. Encourage your partner and assist each other in calling balls which may be going out of bounds and in deciding who should take the down-the-middle shot by saying "mine" or "yours."

9. Get the ball in play. Double faults and careless errors prevent success and enjoyment of the game.

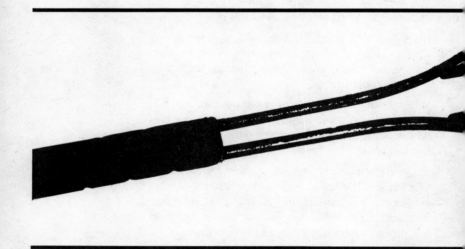

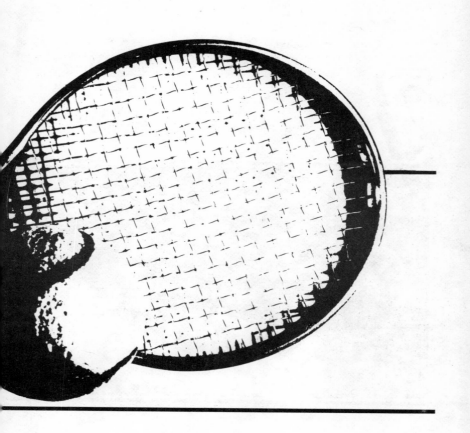

7

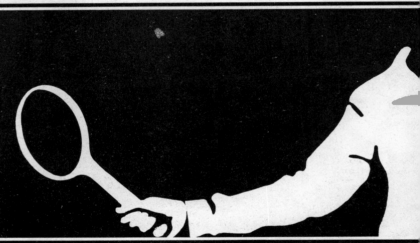

MEASURING IMPROVEMENT AND ACHIEVEMENT

ASSESSING PLAYING ABILITY AND LEVEL OF SKILL

Before learning a new motor skill through self-instruction or with the aid of a professional instructor, it is important to have a general idea of your present level of skill, physical conditioning, and general motor ability.

There are few, if any, meaningful ways to test the level of skill geared to the pace of actual tennis play. As mentioned before, beginners usually fall into one of three categories: (1) those who have never played or held a racket before, (2) those who have played, but without instruction or attention given to correct grips, footwork, etc., and (3) those who have played a little with occasional help from a friend or instructor. The consistency with which one executes the basic strokes (service and forehand, and backhand drives) at the normal pace with evidence of acceptable patterns of strategy enables the player or instructor to arrive at a reasonable decision as to which level of skill the learner represents.

IMPROVEMENT

Once the level of skill has been determined, the next step is a plan for improvement. It is proposed that this improvement is greatly influenced in two ways: (1) through use of drills to improve a particular stroke, and (2) through a good physical-conditioning program which emphasizes exercises that aid in conditioning for the actual playing situations.

The following sequence of drills is suggested for improvement in the forehand and backhand drives:

1. On command, assume the ready position, pivot, racket back, transfer weight as contact with imaginary ball is made, follow through, and move back to correct ready position for the next ball. Practice this for both the forehand and backhand drives.

2. Assume the playing position on the baseline and have a friend or the instructor toss balls to both the forehand and the backhand. If one is available, a machine which projects balls at the normal playing pace is effective.

3. Assume the correct position for hitting a forehand stroke (front foot forward and left shoulder to the net), drop a ball, and hit it. Reverse this for the backhand.

4. Prior to volleying or practicing in a normal playing position on the baseline, stand on the service line and hit the ball gently from mid-court to an opponent who is standing at mid-court on the opposite side. This gives one time to concentrate on changing grips, pivoting, and working on the backswing and follow-through.

5. Assume the regular playing position near the baseline for rallying during the practice of the forehand and backhand strokes.

6. Hit against the backboard at varying distances. This furnishes a consistent ball to practice against.

After these steps have been successfully accomplished, drills to practice cross-court and down-the-line forehand and backhand drives are helpful in the development of sound ground strokes.

These steps have been found to be particularly successful for improvement of the forehand and the backhand drives. However, individuals will usually devise and select a variety of additional aids.

The following drills are suggested as aids in improving the service:

1. To increase strength in the arm and shoulder (1) practice the service motion with a 3- to 5-lb. weight — less for girls, (2) squeeze a rubber ball or start at the corner of a newspaper and wad it up gradually to increase strength in the fingers and the wrist.

2. If you are experiencing difficulty with the entire motion of the service, eliminate all aspects of the motion except where the racket has been drawn behind the head as if you were going to scratch your back. Now the extension of the arm and racket, the contact of the ball, and follow-through have become natural; start again, adding the beginning motion.

3. The toss of the ball is very important in the execution of a good service. Practice the toss without hitting the ball. Leave the tossing hand extended and catch the ball several times.

THE SIX MOST COMMON FAULTS AND WHAT TO DO ABOUT THEM[1]

The aim of every tennis player, whatever his level, is to improve. The two factors that determine improvement are knowledge and practice. If you practice two hours a day but don't understand how to hit the ball, you can compound your errors until they become bad habits that are hard to break. If you understand how to hit the ball but never practice, your arm, feet, eyes, body, and mind will not react to the moving ball. You may be guilty of two, four, or perhaps all six of the errors most

[1]Adapted from an article by Gladys M. Heldman, "The Six Most Common Faults and What To Do About Them." World Tennis, January, 1978, pp. 46-50.

commonly found in tennis. If you can recognize the errors in your game and are willing to work, you can make the correction.

Late Preparation

The most common mistake, particularly at the beginner and intermediate level, is late preparation. Whereas the champion makes his move the instant the ball leaves the opponent's racket, the novice does not take his racket back until the ball has bounced. Intermediates generally start the backswing as the ball is coming over the net. Good players almost always prepare early, but when they find themselves matched against better players they are often late. The harder the ball is hit, the more vital it is to prepare instantaneously.

THE CORRECTION. Stand in front of a mirror with your racket held in the ready position. Your knees should be flexed. Pretend a ball is coming to your forehand: keep your eyes on the mirror but turn your shoulders to the right, with both hands on the racket. If you turn your shoulders properly, your weight will automatically shift to your right foot and the racket will be by your side or slightly farther back. You are now in position to hit the ball in front of you. Come back to the ready position and pretend a ball is coming to your backhand. Your shoulders immediately move to the left, and once again you are ready to hit the ball in front of you. Repeat the drill a hundred times. Make the reaction automatic.

When you first try the shoulder turn on the court, your brain will send a delayed signal to your body. The opponent hits the ball over the net, but your legs and arms do not react. What you were able to do in front of the mirror you are unable to do on the court. However, if you continue to work on turning instantaneously, your brain will begin to signal more quickly. You may fail on the first 20 attempts; the ball actually bounces before your shoulders can rotate. Within 10 minutes, your reactions will speed up, although you may be turning properly only one time in 8 hits. After four or five sessions you will be preparing more rapidly. When you are able to hit 10 balls out of 10 without being late, you are no longer a beginner.

Early preparation is the key to winning tennis. Chris Evert has the fastest shoulder turn in the game.

Wiggling on Service

The mark of the novice is the wiggling that distorts the balance on the service motion. Beginners develop an assortment of odd body movements, including bending from the waist, throwing the hips backward at the hit, allowing the swing of the arms to sway the body, dipping the head, splaying the knees outward, etc. Bending the knees before the toss, describing a wide arc with the toss arm, or bowing as though in the presence of royalty are traits of the untrained player. They "see" body motion on serve among tournament players and perhaps the conclusion they draw is that any body motion, no matter how awkward, is better than none. Unfortunately, wiggles prevent the serve from having accuracy and power.

THE CORRECTION. Remove all wiggles, bends, and bows. There should be one motion only, which will be the transfer of weight from the back foot forward. Start the service motion with the weight on the right (back) foot. As the ball is tossed, the weight remains on the back foot; there has been absolutely no body motion other than the lifting of the left arm and the backward rotation of the right arm. As the right arm comes forward from the back-scratching position, the weight moves to the front foot. The right arm and shoulder swing through on the hit and, in the process, the right foot may come into the court, with the weight transferring to the forward foot.

The correct shoulder-and-arm movement is what causes the weight transfer. The movement does not come from the hips. Unless you are already a tournament player, forget about knee and back action: the action you attempt to add to your serve may actually detract from its power.

You will never be able to dispense with wiggles and achieve good weight transfer if your toss is not precise. If the toss motion is smooth and accurate, you won't have to "chase" the ball in order to hit it. Sometimes the excessive body motion comes from trying to make contact with an errant toss.

Failure to Follow Through

Although almost every teaching pro encourages a full follow-through, many intermediates fall into the terrible habit of stopping the swing immediately after the hit. This is a "fear" reaction: if the player has been hitting wildly, his unconscious mind directs him to cut the swing short to prevent the ball from sailing out. Of course, the exact opposite occurs. The player who stops the swing in the middle will generally open the racket face, particularly on the forehand, and the ball shoots forward without control.

THE CORRECTION. Hit the ball well in front of your body, making sure your shoulders are turned. You may fail to follow through because your body is squarely facing the net. If you step forward (with your left foot on a forehand or your right foot on a backhand) just before the moment of impact, it makes it easier and more natural to finish the stroke. Now your arm can swing through freely, finishing well above your shoulder and pointing to the top of the opponent's fence. The occasions that make it most difficult to follow through are when you take the ball late or when both shoulders face the net.

Hitting from the Elbow on the Backhand

The pivot point on a proper backhand is the shoulder. However, the player with a defensive or weak backhand almost always has the elbow as his pivot point. This means he is getting no body weight into the shot; the power can come only from the forearm and/or wrist. There are occasions, particularly on touch shots, when one can hit a pretty good "elbow" backhand, but 99 percent of players will not be able to hit deep, accurate backhand drives if the elbow is the pivot point.

THE CORRECTION. Stand in front of a mirror in the ready position, but without a racket. Let your left hand grip your right hand. Your left hand will now pull your right arm straight back; you are still facing the mirror but your left shoulder has swung all the way around and your right shoulder is pointing at the looking-glass. The right arm is slightly bent. Now let the left hand drop. Swing your right arm forward and up, with your shoulder acting as the pivot point. At no point does the elbow ever "lead" as you swing your arm.

As your left hand pulls your right arm back, you will feel the pull in your shoulder. Just before you swing the right arm forward, take a step toward the mirror with your right foot. When the right arm swings forward, there is no movement of the elbow; the rotation is totally from the shoulder.

When you try your new backhand on the court, take the ball well in front of your body. If you take the ball late (by your side), the old tendency to hit from the elbow may recur. As with all new strokes, it is best to practice against soft or short shots to give yourself plenty of time.

Facing the Net on Forehand

Players who have weak forehands almost always face the net on the hit. Players with excellent forehands invariably turn the shoulder. It is not possible to drive a forehand accurately if both shoulders are parallel to the net. A weak forehand can become a powerful and controlled weapon simply by getting the shoulder around in plenty of time.

THE CORRECTION. The easiest way to guarantee the shoulder turn is to keep the left hand on the racket and let the left hand push the right hand back. As soon as the left hand has done the pushing, you are in position to hit the ball. Once the shoulder is turned, you can step forward and meet the ball well in front of the body.

Planting the Feet

Inexperienced players are invariably flat-footed. The better players hop and bounce. If you watch Guillermo Vilas on television, you see him hopping and bouncing as much in the fifth set as in the first. If you want to move quickly, you must be bouncy. As the eye registers where the ball is going, the feet should start moving. If you are playing on clay and the ball takes a bad bounce, you must be light enough on your feet to hop forward or back. The player with planted feet cannot start quickly enough nor can he adjust immediately to a crazy spin or a bad bounce.

THE CORRECTION. There are two exercises that, in particular, will help you to develop better footwork. One is skipping sideways: five skips to the left, then five skips to the right. Skip sideways on the court to get into position or to adjust to a bounce or to get to a ball that is reasonably close. The skip is what gives you the ability to make last-minute adjustments. The second exercise is pushing off on one foot to run in the opposite direction. If you want to move quickly to the left, let your full weight come down on your right foot: the right knee bends, then the right foot pushes off, and away you skip. Your weight comes down on your right heel just before you push off.

Your feet must react as your eye sees the ball. As the opponent hits, the eye sees the ball come off the racket and, simultaneously, one foot pushes off. The earlier you see the ball and the bouncier you are, the more quickly you move.

NOVEL PRACTICE DRILLS AND GAMES

The following games and drills can be played by either beginning, intermediate, or advanced players. Special adaptations of these drills may be made for players whose developing skills prohibit them from playing the games and drills as they are described.[2]

[2]Permission to adapt and quote from Ed Collins' article, "Tips on Tennis" in the May 1972 issue of *World Tennis*, pp. 60-64, was graciously extended by Mrs. Gladys Heldman, editor and publisher of *World Tennis*.

"21"

This is a game played from the baseline. The player starts the ball with a ground stroke. The ball must be hit three times; the fourth hit starts the point. This is the "3-hit rule." The players remain at the baseline and exchange ground strokes until someone errs. They may not rush the net. Drop shots, therefore, are not allowed and are played again.

Scoring: The first player reaching 21 points wins.

Purpose: To develop steady baseline play; "21" will help the player who normally tends to choke up under pressure of a long point.

"31 Vasss"

The ping-pong scoring method is applied to tennis. The players alternate service after 5 points, changing sides every 10 points. A match consists of 31 points, but a player must win by 2 points.

"Percentage Tennis"

This is an all-court game (serve, ground strokes, volley) where a player wins three points each time his opponent sends the ball into the net or outside the boundary lines, two points if the opponent double-faults, and one point if he hits a good shot (a winner or a forced error) that his opponent fails to return.

Scoring: 31 points.

Purpose: To understand and execute percentage tennis.

"Learning to Spin"

Placing his right knee on the court, the player serves the ball from well behind the baseline. This is an excellent elementary drill in teaching the intermediate to spin the ball. From this low position the player must hit up and over the ball in order to reach the service court.

"Short-Court"

Here is a mid-court game where the players hit from within the boundaries of the service court. A player puts the ball into play with an underhand ground-stroke motion while standing behind the service line. The "serve" must be successfully returned or a replay or second serve is required. The players alternate serve after five points.

Scoring: The same as in "31 Vasss."

Purpose: To develop touch and improve drop shots and angle shots. The playing of volleys is optional.

"Deep"

Another baseline game where the player puts the ball into play with a ground stroke. The ball must be hit deep enough to clear the service line. The point is lost if the ball lands short of the service line. The 3-hit rule, whereby the ball must cross the net three times, is used (the fourth hit starts the point).

"Crosscourt"

A player puts the ball into play with a ground stroke. The players attempt to maintain a continuous crosscourt rally. The 3-hit rule is used. All shots must go cross-court.

Scoring: For drill, play to a specified number of points.

Purpose: To develop confidence in the forehand and backhand cross-court drives.

"Down-the-Line"

A player starts the ball with a ground stroke. The players attempt to maintain a continuous rally down-the-line. The 3-hit rule is used.

Scoring: Play to 11 points hitting forehands, then change and play backhands to 11.

Purpose: To develop confidence in the forehand and backhand down-the-line drives.

"Hit and Volley"

One player positions himself at the service line while another player stands at net. The service-line player starts the play with a ground stroke. The 3-hit rule is used. Play is restricted to the boundaries created by the service court.

Scoring: For drill, play to a specified number of points.

Purpose: To develop beginning volley skill. Players should learn to block the ball for reliable results. Shorter backswing is necessary for the block.

"Pass 'em If You Can"

This is a volley practice game where one player is on the baseline and the other is at net. Baseline play introduces the ball into play with a ground stroke. The 3-hit rule is used. Boundary: half the court or the full court (width). The ground-stroker attempts to force an error from the net player by hitting past or through the net player. A player may not lob.

Scoring: For drill or play to a specified number of points.

Purpose: To develop advanced skills in the volley.

"Pepper Volley"

One player stands at the service line and sends five balls, one immediately after another, at the net player, who attempts to return each.

Purpose: Developing fast reactions at net.

"Developing a Harder Serve"

The player stands as close to the fence as his swing will allow and attempts to hit his serve from fence to fence. Through repetitive practice this will help strengthen the shoulder and develop a faster serve.

"Madness"

Two players stand at opposite sides of the net at the service line and exchange volleys, stepping forward with each shot until they meet at the edge of the net and catch the ball in the air.

Purpose: Fun.

"Closing"

Two players position themselves on opposite sides of the net, one at the baseline and the other at the service line. The baseline player puts the ball into play with a ground stroke to the net player, who volleys the ball. The baseline player then hits the ball where the net player can hit a forehand volley followed by a backhand volley. The objective is to play either of the volleys for a winner.

Purpose: An exercise in closing in on the volley.

"2 on 1"

Player A serves five points to players B and C. A plays into the doubles court while the doubles team plays into the singles court. Players rotate serve after every five points.

Variation: A serves to B while C plays net on B's side. A serves five points and then joins B while C plays alone. The players continue to rotate, each serving to one another. Each player keeps his own score. The first to reach 31 points wins the game.

"Controlled Smash"

This is a game to develop the lob and overhead. The players pair up, one sending lobs, and the other playing a controlled overhead. The player executing the lob must stand behind the baseline. The players attempt to maintain a lob-overhead sequence.

Scoring: Count the number of consecutive overheads in a given time period.

Purpose: To develop a sure and consistent overhead and improve skills in the lob.

"Boom"

Here is another practice game for the lob and overhead. One team assumes the net position while the other plays from the baseline. One baseliner puts the ball into play by sending a ground stroke to the netmen, who volley the ball deep to the baseline. The point is then in play as the baseliners try to lob over the netmen. If they are successful, the net players must try to regain their position at the net. The baseline players may only play lobs.

Scoring: For drill, or play to 21 points.

Variation: Four players (two netmen, two baseliners) play against a doubles team at the baseline.

Purpose: To develop lob and overhead skills.

"Hitting the Corners"

Make a pyramid of balls (three balls touching, with one resting on top) and place them in the extreme far corners of the service court. Players then attempt to break the pyramid through repetitive service practice.

"Serve and Run"

Team members serve 20 balls each at 3/4 speed or with spin serves. For each fault the server must run one lap around the inside of the court. It is an excellent drill for the player who tends to choke up on his second serve. It is also good for the lazy player and develops concentration and conditioning.

"Lob Rally"

This is a practice game for the lob. Two or four players exchange lobs from the baseline, attempting to keep the ball deep beyond the service line.

Scoring: For drill, or play to a specified number of points.

Purpose: To develop skills in executing a lob.

SPORTS MEDICINE FOR ATHLETES

The athlete of the 1980s is the young man or woman involved in learning a skill in one or more lifetime sports such as tennis, golf, cycling, and so on.

Athletes in these sports — in our case, tennis — require medical attention in order to participate free of injury. In tennis, you should give special attention to two areas.

The first area is that of strength/flexibility. Strength was always thought to be of major importance to the tennis player. Now, flexibility has moved alongside in terms of importance. Flexibility is necessary in order to prevent muscle pulls, strains, and tears, and also to prevent abnormal stress in the arches, shoulders, elbows, and certain other body areas.

The second area is the feet. With the development of podiatry (the study of foot disorders), it has been discovered that injury to the feet can cause troubles in the legs, knees, thighs, and lower back. Obviously, all these body areas are important to the tennis player.

The explosion of new tennis equipment, types of shoes, playing surfaces, and rackets all enter into the analysis of tennis players medical fitness and their ability to play free from injury.

PHYSICAL CONDITIONING

No matter how skilled the player becomes in making sound strokes, if the optimum level of physical fitness is not attained and maintained, the overall performance will be greatly affected. A well planned conditioning program gives general attention to overall conditioning and special attention to conditioning for actual play.

A sound program which develops overall conditioning and endurance includes a 3- to 5-mile distance each day, alternating the speed from a sprint, to a brisk jog, to a brisk walking pace, and then repeating the cycle. Specific exercises to increase strength, agility, and coordination include: finger-tip push-ups, sit-ups, bicycling, kangaroo jumps, rope-jumping, and light weight lifting (3 to 7 lbs.) which are used to overload in particular motions like serving (use the weight instead of a racket).

In addition, practicing from a ready position the footwork, backswing, and follow-through of each stroke at a speeded-up pace is helpful, as well as extended rallies where one player is at the net and the other is at the baseline, are highly beneficial. These positions are reversed after an exchange of a predetermined amount of balls. Particular areas or shots to be practiced should be designated in advance.

The best conditioning program is one which is geared to actual playing conditions and to movements on the court during actual play. Design a program that not only improves your strong features but also detects and strengthens your weak points. For help in designing your program, consult a specialist in athletic coaching or a physical education instructor.

EVALUATION OF ACHIEVEMENT

Achievement or progress must be recognizable or one soon loses interest. It is possible to become accomplished in areas other than playing skill and this should be taken into consideration. As your playing ability improves you should have:

1. recognized the value of tennis as a part of one's total educational experiences, which may enrich one's whole life;

2. acquired social competencies which are becoming in a competitive situation involving either men or women or both;

3. recognized the value of tennis as a means by which emotional tensions are released and a refreshed mental attitude results.

The three aforementioned areas of evaluation almost defy actual testing and probably do not need formal test proceedings. However, certain tests which reveal achievement in the acquiring of skill are of great value to the learner.

Prior to testing actual skill, an evaluation of physical achievement should be conducted.

Can you:

1. alternately walk, jog, and sprint at least three miles without feeling rubbery-legged, without gasping for breath, or without suffering sharp pains in the abdomen?

2. play five sets of tennis and not feel sore and stiff the following day?

3. play five sets of vigorous tennis and feel relatively fresh or only normally fatigued at the end?

4. Is each particular muscular area which is especially taxed in tennis specifically conditioned to the level so that it is not sore or strained after a long match, e.g., the serving wrist, the lower back?

TESTING YOUR SKILLS

The ways in which individual skill can be measured include: (1) a subjective rating of form by the individual player or an observer, (2) the ability to rally against a more highly skilled player or the backboard, (3) the results of a competitive tournament (although here factors involved in match play interfere with measurement of a particular stroke), and (4) the player's skill in placing the ball in designated areas of the court at the normal pace of actual play.

Specific tests of skill for beginners include:

1. Hit balls forehand and backhand from a stationary position into designated areas of the court. Speed, angle, accuracy, consistency, and depth of the shot indicate the level of skill. The balls to be hit may be projected from a machine or tossed by another person. A rope should be stretched parallel to the net at approximately 3' or 4' in height. The ball should pass between the rope and the top of the net.

2. Hit balls as in No. 1 but include the pivot and step toward the ball.

3. As skill progresses, the same tests may be employed against an opponent while rallying or in a match.

4. Testing the service can be done in a similar fashion. How many balls can you hit into a designated area of the court, at a normal playing pace for beginners? Test yourself on both the flat and twist services.

As you advance in skill and new strokes are introduced, similar methods for assessing achievement may be devised. There are two additional skills not involved in actual play which beginners should learn. These are: (1) between points when your opponent hits the ball to you (e.g., you are serving) learn to place the racket out with a closed face and stop the ball, and (2) learn to tap the ball when it is lying on the court with the face of the racket and pick it up.

It is extremely important that you be able to determine in one or several of the ways mentioned your level of skill when you begin to learn to play, and that you make frequent checks by one of these means to determine your rate of progress. This will enable you to set new goals and maintain your interest and desire to improve and play.

BEYOND BASIC SKILLS

Being able to execute the service and forehand and backhand drives constitute the basic skills of tennis. After this the beginner should learn the volley, lob, and overhead smash, and perhaps a variety of shots which include the drop shot and drop volley, slice, chop, and half-volley.

Your game still needs bolstering by attention to a few ideas and attitudes toward involvements during play and spectating. Let us consider some of these.

PLACEMENT, CONSISTENCY, POWER: MENTAL STRATEGY

You may have seen players at the various levels of skill who had tremendous power or force on their shots, but never got the ball in the desired part of the court. You also may have seen players who could dink the ball back and forth in an endless rally but without winning enough points to win a game or match. And then, you may have seen players who were forceful and consistent but could not place the ball in the area of the court they desired.

It is usually accepted that consistency and placement win most rallies and matches. However, the power shot should not be overlooked. A common mistake in attempting to hit a power drive or volley is too much wrist snap or "whipping" of the ball. Increased power on the drive and the volley is best accomplished by keeping the wrist firm, by hitting the ball well in front of the body, and by transferring the weight from the back foot into the ball at the point of contact. Topspin and underspin should be avoided since both diminish power. The racket face should be flat, the back fairly straight, and a good backswing and follow-through are essential. Avoid a stiff arm motion.

To increase power on the service, the ball should be tossed to the height of the extended arm and racket and contacted at that height with a good wrist snap upon the completion of the hit. The forward motion of the arm, shoulder, and hips are important in the production of a powerful service. A combination of placement, consistency, and power are all usually needed to achieve higher levels of skill.

THE DEVELOPMENT OF AGILITY AND QUICKNESS

Accompanying sound execution of basic strokes is the development of quickness or agility. The following factors influence this development: reflexes, anticipation, eye-hand coordination, and general mobility of body movement.

Basic considerations when attempting to improve quickness or agility include:

1. Attempt to see the ball as it contacts the opponent's racket.

2. Develop appropriate level of strength and endurance in specific areas of the body upon which one must rely, e.g., the wrist. If the wrist is weak or tires easily, the quickness in which the player positions his racket and the power of the stroke produced is actually decreased.

3. Correct footwork and general body mobility are essential to quick movement. Practicing lunging feints, returning to correct ready position, and movements required in normal play situations aid in the improvement of reactions involved in good footwork and body mobility.

Essentially, quickness of reflexes is a product of mental reaction. Seeing the ball early, and reacting by moving in the anticipated direction of your opponent's return, should lead you closer to your highest playing potential.

THE ART OF SPECTATING

Being a good tennis player but a poor tennis spectator is a paradox which should not exist. It frequently does. Particularly at the beginning stage, observing others play can aid in the improvement of your individual game. Concentrate on one player, and watch all of his movements instead of trying to watch the ball and both players as well.

More important on the long-range basis, perhaps, is the sheer enjoyment of watching a contest in which two or four players use all of their mental and physical abilities to produce a winning game. This is an enjoyable experience which may be individual or shared with friends and family.

Good spectatorship results from knowledge of the game and a consideration for all persons involved in the match, other spectators as well. During play one should avoid movements or verbal distractions which tend to interfere with play. At the conclusion of a good shot or the end of a long rally, applause for both players is always appropriate and usually stimulates the participants and serves as a needed emotional release for the spectator.

After both players have toweled off while changing courts, generous applause should follow their return to play. Respect for the umpire's requests for silence and for his decisions are requisites of the good spectator.

Good sportsmanship has always been a tradition in tennis. This tradition enriches both the playing situation and the spectator's observations.

GOOD MATCH MANNERS

For the fullest enjoyment while playing tennis, both the written and unwritten rules of the game must be observed. Regardless of whether the match is an informal social encounter or a regular tournament match, these hints are always in good taste:

1. Dress according to the club's or playing center's rules.

2. Be punctual for your play.

3. Vacate the court immediately if there is a time regulation.

4. Do not walk behind a court where play is in progress until the point is finished.

5. Ask politely for a ball which has entered another court, by saying "Thank you, please."

6. Stop play immediately if a ball enters your playing area and retrieve it for your neighbor.

7. The server should keep the score accurately and verbally.

8. Take responsibility for calling your individual errors if an umpire is not available, e.g., balls hit on the second bounce, hitting the net with the racket.

9. Do not ask spectators to render decisions.

10. Balls which bounce so close to the line that a decision is difficult should be replayed or given to the opponent.

11. Make decisions on balls which could be questionable quickly and fairly.

12. Avoid talking during a rally unless it is a subtle suggestion to your doubles partner, e.g., "Out" or "I have the ball."

13. Be patient and considerate with your doubles partner.

14. Remove all waste from the court when play is completed.

15. Respect the decisions of the linesmen, the umpire, and your opponent.

16. Be courteous at the conclusion of your match, regardless of the outcome.

In addition to these suggestions, intuitive reactions during play always indicate the manners of the individual. Ladies and gentlemen are athletes and certainly athletes can be ladies and gentlemen.

9

TENNIS AND THE INDIVIDUAL

VALUES

Philosophical Values

The values of tennis are readily recognized. First, there is simply the value of learning a sport or physical skill, a skill which you can continue to use until you are no longer physically mobile. Second, physical activity such as tennis provides a good balance to an academic course study. Third, playing tennis with confidence and assurance will give you lifelong pleasure. Thus, tennis experience is an important part of the total educational picture.

Physiological Values

After the basic skills have been learned and can be performed at the normal pace of play, tennis can contribute toward the optimum physiological functioning of the human body. A vigorous set of tennis may contribute to increased muscular development, and more efficient cardiovascular, respiratory, and organic functioning, increased arm, leg, and lower trunk strength, agility, coordination, and balance, stamina and endurance, and weight control.

Psychological Values

Most players go to school or work or both. Once this meant a job requiring 8, 10, or even more hours per day, for 6 or 7 days a week. Modern society is experiencing the 40-hour week and in ten years this may be cut in half.

Recently educators and physicians have given attention to the research of the psychological values of participation in physical activities such as tennis. Even though research evidence is lacking to support this theory, it seems safe to assert by observation and conversations with participants that a good vigorous game of tennis may help to release tensions built up by crowded schedules of classes or the work day, assists the player in clarification of his self-image, provides an outlet for anger, frustration, and aggression, lessens the overall feeling of mental confusion which is the result of a busy schedule, and aids the player in returning to reality.

Sociological Values

In a society noted for its pressures and for its spawning of nonconformists and isolationists, there is an ever-increasing need for opportunities providing congenial social outlets. Tennis meets this need. Tennis provides an opportunity for people to get together formally and informally and enjoy learning a physical skill in an all-male, all-female, or coeducational setting. It provides players with the opportunity to make new friends and enjoy a wholesome competitive experience. It provides an opportunity for practicing good manners and sportsmanship, for gaining experience in acceptable verbal interchange in competitive situations, and for practicing self-discipline and control of the emotions in both winning and losing situations. It may also provide an opportunity to practice cooperation and to develop empathy and self-confidence in an individual or group situation.

Economic Values

The choice of tennis as a professional sports career now ranks higher than golf and its top participants are equal to athletes in the other established professional sports. Today, many young men and women are setting their goals in life to include a lucrative tour career.

While a few look to the big-money scene, even more are selecting the teaching of tennis — in schools, colleges-universities, private clubs, housing centers, recreation centers, and even in situations supplementary to their main job — as a career choice. So, tennis has arrived as a legitimate professional career option as a teacher/coach or a tournament competitor.

EDUCATION OF THE WHOLE MAN

The most important considerations for you, the individual player, are your self-image and the unfolding of your potential in an attempt to become the best individual that you may possibly become. Perhaps the second most important consideration is your personal concept of mankind in general and your relationship with your fellow man. Thus, a clear conception of the nature of man and his potential is necessary if one is to become a totally educated individual. Needs and abilities are complex. Needs must be identified and abilities developed.

Even though there is some disagreement as to the oneness of personality, it is my contention that the central emphasis in life should be placed upon the unity of the total person and that the interdependence of all aspects of self be recognized and accepted. An attempt to divide man into physical, psychological, social, and spiritual components is meaningless unless we realize their mutual interdependence. Hence, the attempt to actualize your individual potential and aid in making you as wholly educated a man as possible is a very worthy goal. Include in it experiences which contribute to your attaining your highest level of vibrant health, skill, joy, and creative use. Tennis can be such an experience!

SUGGESTED READINGS

CLASSICS

Buchanan, Lamont. *The Story of Tennis.* New York: Vanguard Press, 1951.

Budge, J. Donald. *Budge on Tennis.* Englewood Cliffs, NJ: Prentice-Hall, 1949.

Budge, Lloyd. *Tennis Made Easy.* New York: The Ronald Press, 1945.

Connolly, Maureen. *Championship Tennis.* London: Muller, 1954.

Gibson, Althea. *I Always Wanted to Be Somebody.* New York: Harper, 1958. A heartwarming biography with sociological implications.

Potter, Ned. *Kings of the Court.* New York: A. S. Barnes, 1963. The history of tennis.

POPULAR READING

Play Tennis With Rosewall. 160 pp., illus., 1976. Essentially an instructional book, it also includes Rosewall's tennis philosophy. Covers all the strokes as well as common errors and corrections for them. Includes chapters on psychology and strategy, dealing with tennis variables, and biographies of other famous players.

Psychology of Sport: The Behavior, Motivation, Personality, and Performance of Athletes by Dorcas Susan Butt. 196 pp., illus., 1976. A thought-provoking analysis of the psychological dynamics of sports. Describes how athletes' motivations reflect the values of contemporary society as well as the psychology of individual players. Sex role conflicts are examined and the social structure of organized sports analyzed. Evaluates the benefit of mental discipline, hypnosis, and coaching and provides guidelines that will prove most effective in developing athletic competence.

Inner Tennis by W. Timothy Gallwey. 173 pp., 1976. Based on a simple concept — that the key to winning tennis lies inside every player's head, in his ability to concentrate, to let his game just "happen." Provides detailed mental and physical exercises in self-mastery.

Tennis Equipment by Steve Fiott. 125 pp., illus., 1976. This unique guide provides all you need to know about tennis gear. Thoroughly describes the construction of the different types of tennis rackets, shoes, balls and strings. Includes an impartial, detailed analysis and the performance expectations of each piece of equipment.

FITNESS AND HEALTH

Conditioning Exercises (as suggested by Margaret Court) 3 pp., 1974. Exercises for stretching, speed, footwork, strength, and stamina.

PERIODICALS

World Tennis. CBS Publications Inc., Marion, OH. Published monthly. Gives tournament results and teaching hints.

INSTRUCTIONAL MATERIAL FOR THE PLAYER, TEACHER AND COACH

Advanced Tennis for Coaches, Teachers, and Players by Gundars A. Tilmanis. 126 pp., illus., 1975. Drawing upon his knowledge of diomechanics, and illustrated by more than 200 photos, the author comprehensively analyzes the techniques of stroke production and outlines a teaching progression for the instructor. Lesson plans contain many innovative teaching devices, exercises, and methods of analyzing weaknesses.

Advantage Tennis by John M. Barnaby (a revision of *Racket Work*). 250 pp., illus., 1975. Emphasis on the idea that the key to tennis is skillful racket work. Covers the basic strokes, advanced shots, and strategy and tactics for singles and doubles play. Includes a special section on coaching and teaching tennis.

Ed Faulkner's Tennis: How to Play It, How to Teach It by Ed Faulkner and Fred Weymuller. 294 pp., illus., 1970. Detailed analysis of each stroke; drills and experiences that lead to confidence and mastery; and a description of frequent trouble spots and how to overcome them.

Inside Tennis by Jim Leighton. 192 pp., illus., 1977. A sound text on tennis strokes and strategy, with various sections written by eight outstanding teaching pros: Pauline Betz Addie, Bill Lufler, Bill Murphy, Chet Murphy, Wayne Sabin, Welby Van Horn, Dennis Van der Meer, and Jim Leighton. Covers material for all levels of players — beginner, intermediate, advanced. Excellent reading for both the player and for the teacher.

Tennis by Elaine Mason. 146 pp., illus., 1974. Presents "Graduated Length Method" approach to learning tennis, and describes numerous "learning experiences" for readers to practice. Includes sections on strategy, rules, court etiquette, conditioning, practice skills, and a brief history of the game.

Tennis: The Bassett System by Glenn Bassett. 106 pp., illus., 1977. The coach of powerhouse UCLA tennis teams and top stars such as Connors and Ashe outlines his techniques for teaching tennis. Included are all the secrets and inside tips he has used through the years. Bassett explains his easily learned four-step system of stroke production. Every stroke is broken down, analyzed, and explained in detail. Also includes chapters on practice techniques and strategy.

Tennis for the Future by Vic Braden and Bill Bruns. 274 pp., illus., 1977. A unique text-and-picture guide which combines Braden's experience, expertise, warmth, and wit. Covers all the basic strokes, tactics, practice drills, conditioning, and self-evaluation check-points. In addition, contains excellent material on how to develop confidence, how to perform well under pressure, and how to master a no-frills approach to strategy.

STRATEGY

The Complete Pocket Tennis Strategist by Donald Sonneman.
56 pp., illus., 1974. A small handbook you can place in the
pocket of your tennis shorts to guide you as you play.
Provides the overall game plan for singles and doubles.
Details and tactics used to implement the appropriate
strategy.

The Game of Doubles in Tennis by William F. Talbert and
Bruce S. Old. 214 pp., illus., 1977. Contains 112 diagrams
of court strategy and team play. Includes a thorough
analysis of the most successful plays in specific situations,
and instruction in the serve, return of service, net play, and
baseline play.

The Game of Singles in Tennis by William F. Talbert and
Bruce S. Old. 158 pp., illus., 1977. A tactics and strategy
book. Based on the premise that there is a defense for
every attack and an attack for every defense. Strokes are
explained, analyzed, and demonstrated. Illustrated
diagrams included.

Match Play and the Spin of the Ball by Bill Tilden. 177 pp.,
illus., 1969. A classic text for the serious amateur who is
ready to learn some of the fine points of analysis and ball
control. Tilden's theories on match play and spin describe
those ingredients which are absolutely essential for
successful competitive tennis.

Use Your Head in Tennis by Bob Harmon with Keith Monroe.
230 pp., illus., 1978. Bob Harmon teaches you how to beat
better players using tested techniques. Describes all the
angles, the fine points, and the subtleties that enable a
smart player to beat an inferior one, even when the lesser
player happens to be able to run faster and hit harder.
Includes description of the basic strokes, ball control,
anticipation, singles and doubles play.

*Winning with Percentage Tennis: An Expert's Guide to Smart
Court Strategy* by Jack Lowe. 92 pp., illus., 1974.
Percentage tennis is described as eliminating the desire to
try the one great shot, instead working toward consistency.
In addition to discussing percentage tennis strategy for both
singles and doubles play, Lowe also presents a stroke
analysis which is simple enough for beginners yet detailed
enough for advanced players.

Note: Names of publishers may be obtained by writing to *World Tennis*.

PEFORMANCE CHECK LIST

How to Use the Evaluation Forms

The forms that follow were designed to be used in a variety of instructional settings. Planning and organization are necessary for these devices to be used as effectively as possible. The purpose of evaluation is to gauge how well the course objectives are accomplished. That is, evaluation will indicate the progress and the extent to which learning has occurred.

Although the learner *must do his own learning,* the instructor's role is to guide and to direct learning experiences and to provide for appropriate measurement procedures. The charts that follow have been constructed to place primary responsibility on the learner for estimating progress, and to indicate areas that need work. It may not be either necessary or desirable to use all the materials provided here in a given teaching/learning situation. The instructor and player should work together to select the materials most appropriate for learning.

It must be remembered that sufficient time for practice and study must be provided if the player is to perfect his skills as well accrue knowledge and to develop understanding. The time available may not be adequate for *all* players to demonstrate acceptable levels of skill performance. The instructor may wish to supplement the evaluation devices with a written test covering analysis of performance, procedures, and rules. The written test provides an opportunity for the player to demonstrate his knowledge and understanding of the skill even though his actual skill might be less than desired. Final evaluation for grading purposes should take into account a number of variables that may have an influence on individual performance.

Practice _____

Player _____

Instructor _____

Date _____

PLAYER	FOREHAND	INSTRUCTOR
_____	Accuracy	_____
_____	Power	_____
_____	Depth	_____
_____	Spin	_____
_____	Top	_____
_____	Slice	_____
_____	Cross-court	_____
_____	Down-the-line	_____
_____	Drop Shot	_____
_____	Passing Shot	_____
_____	**Lob**	
_____	Offensive	_____
_____	Defensive	_____
_____	TOTAL EFFICIENCY	_____
	BACKHAND	
_____	Accuracy	_____
_____	Power	_____
_____	Depth	_____
_____	Spin	_____
_____	Top	_____
_____	Slice	_____
_____	Cross-court	_____
_____	Down-the-line	_____
_____	Drop Shot	_____
_____	Passing Shot	_____

Practice _____

Player _____

Instructor _____

Date _____

PLAYER   **INSTRUCTOR**

_____   **Lob**   _____

_____   Offensive   _____

_____   Defensive   _____

_____   TOTAL EFFICIENCY   _____

                              SERVES

                               Flat

_____   Depth   _____

_____   Accuracy   _____

_____   Spin   _____

_____   Power   _____

_____   TOTAL EFFICIENCY   _____

                               Spin

_____   Depth   _____

_____   Accuracy   _____

_____   Spin   _____

_____   Power   _____

_____   TOTAL EFFICIENCY   _____

                               Slice

_____   Depth   _____

_____   Accuracy   _____

_____   Spin   _____

_____   Power   _____

_____   TOTAL EFFICIENCY   _____

Practice _____

Player _____

Instructor _____

Date _____

PLAYER	**VOLLEY**	**INSTRUCTOR**
	Forehand	
_____	Depth	_____
_____	Accuracy	_____
_____	Power	_____
_____	Speed	_____
_____	Height Over Net	_____
_____	TOTAL EFFICIENCY	_____
	Backhand	
_____	Depth	_____
_____	Accuracy	_____
_____	Power	_____
_____	Speed	_____
_____	Spin	_____
_____	Height Over Net	_____
_____	TOTAL EFFICIENCY	_____
	TROUBLE SHOTS	
	Half-Volley	
_____	Accuracy	_____
_____	Depth	_____
_____	Height Over Net	_____
_____	Power	_____
_____	Speed	_____
_____	Spin	_____
_____	TOTAL EFFICIENCY	_____

Practice _____

Player _____

Instructor _____

Date _____

PLAYER	Overhead	INSTRUCTOR
_____	Accuracy	_____
_____	Depth	_____
_____	Power	_____
_____	Backcourt	_____
_____	Bounce	_____
_____	Forecourt	_____
_____	Bounce	
	TOTAL EFFICIENCY	_____

SERVICE RECEPTION

Forehand

PLAYER		INSTRUCTOR
_____	Accuracy	_____
_____	Depth	_____
_____	Power	_____
_____	Lob	_____
_____	Offensive	_____
_____	Defensive	_____
_____	Cross-court	_____
_____	Down-the-line	_____
	TOTAL EFFICIENCY	_____

Backhand

PLAYER		INSTRUCTOR
_____	Accuracy	_____
_____	Depth	_____
_____	Power	_____

Practice _____

Player _____

Instructor _____

Date _____

PLAYER		**INSTRUCTOR**
_____	Lob	_____
_____	Offensive	_____
_____	Defensive	_____
_____	Cross-court	_____
_____	Down-the-line	_____
_____	TOTAL EFFICIENCY	_____

SINGLES GENERAL PLAYING STRATEGY

_____	Offensive	_____
_____	Defensive	_____
_____	TOTAL EFFICIENCY	_____

DOUBLES GENERAL PLAYING STRATEGY

_____	Team Player	_____
_____	Offensive	_____
_____	Defensive	_____
_____	TOTAL EFFICIENCY	_____